MW00587510

THE SAVVY INVESTOR'S GUIDE TO BUILDING WEALTH THROUGH ALTERNATIVE INVESTMENTS

THE H. KENT BAKER INVESTMENTS SERIES

THE SAVVY INVESTOR'S GUIDE TO BUILDING WEALTH THROUGH ALTERNATIVE INVESTMENTS

BY

H. KENT BAKER
American University, USA

GREG FILBECK
Penn State Behrend, USA

AND

ANDREW C. SPIELER
Hofstra University, USA

United Kingdom – North America – Japan – India
Malaysia – China

Emerald Publishing Limited
Howard House, Wagon Lane, Bingley BD16 1WA, UK

First edition 2021

Reprints and permissions service
Contact: permissions@emeraldinsight.com

British Library Cataloguing in Publication Data
A catalogue record for this book is available from the British
Library

ISBN: 978-1-80117-138-0 (Print)
ISBN: 978-1-80117-135-9 (Online)
ISBN: 978-1-80117-137-3 (Epub)

ISOQAR certified
Management System,
awarded to Emerald
for adherence to
Environmental
standard
ISO 14001:2004.

Certificate Number 1985
ISO 14001

INVESTOR IN PEOPLE

CONTENTS

LIST OF FIGURES

LIST OF TABLES

ABOUT THE AUTHORS

H. Kent Baker, DBA, PhD, CFA, CMA, is a University Professor of Finance in the Kogod School of Business at American University. He is an award-winning author/editor who has published 38 books and more than 300 articles and other publications. He is among the top 1% of the most prolific authors in finance. He serves on numerous editorial boards and is the editor of two investment book series. He is internationally known for his work in investor behavior, financial markets and investments, and survey research. He has consulting and training experience with more than 100 organizations in the United States, Canada, and Europe. He was the President of the Southern Finance Association and has received numerous research, teaching, and service awards, including the Southern Finance Association's 2019 Distinguished Scholar and American University's Scholar/Teacher of the Year.

Greg Filbeck, DBA, CFA, FRM, CAIA, CIPM, FDP, PRM, holds the Samuel P. Black III Professor of Finance and Risk Management at Penn State Behrend and serves as Director of the Black School of Business. Before joining the faculty at Penn State Behrend in 2006, he served as Senior Vice President of Kaplan Schweser from 1999 to 2006. He also held academic appointments at Miami University (Ohio) and the University of Toledo, where he also served as the Associate Director of the Center for Family Business. He has authored or edited 14 books and published more than 105 refereed academic journal articles. He served as President of the CFA Society Pittsburgh from 2014 to 2018 and was President of the Southern Finance Association from 2015 to 2016.

Andrew C. Spieler, PhD, CFA, FRM, CAIA, is the Robert F. Dall Distinguished Professor of Business and Professor of Finance in the Frank G. Zarb School of Business at Hofstra University. He is the founder of Advanced Quantitative Consulting. He has published over 60 articles, book chapters, and books on real estate, fixed income, hedge funds, and behavioral finance. He received three "Best Paper" awards from the American Real Estate Society. He was also the recipient of two "Distinguished Teacher of the Year" and two "Researcher of the Year" awards at Hofstra University. He is the co-director for the annual conference sponsored by the Breslin Real Estate Center. *The Wall Street Journal, New York Times, MSNBC, ABC News, Fox News*, and others often quote him.

ACKNOWLEDGMENTS AND DEDICATION

"Writing is easy. All you have to do is cross out the wrong words."

Mark Twain

In writing *The Savvy Investor's Guide to Building Wealth Through Alternative Investments*, we kept Mark Twain's comment in mind. Hopefully, we crossed out the wrong words and kept the right ones. However, the publication of this book was a team effort. Everyone at Emerald Publishing involved with this book provided exceptional guidance, especially Charlotte Maiorana (Vice President), Hayley Coulson (Content Development Editor), and Lidiya Prince (Copy Editor). We also owe our respective institutions – the Kogod School of Business at American University, the Black School of Business at Penn State Behrend, and the Frank G. Zarb School of Business at Hofstra University – a debt of gratitude. Finally, we thank our families for their support and understanding: Linda and Rory Baker; Mickey, Judy, Janis, Aaron, Andrea, Kyle, and Grant Filbeck; Terry, Harrison, Teresa, Robin, Kate, and Hudson Spieler.

INTRODUCTION

"Listening to uninformed people is worse than having no answers at all."

Ray Dalio, American Billionaire Investor, Hedge Fund Manager, and Philanthropist

When you think about investing, what types of investments come to mind? Despite the broad range of investment options available, most individual or retail investors usually think of stocks and bonds. You might also keep some savings in a bank or similar instrument, also known as "cash and equivalents," which, along with stocks and bonds, make up the three main asset investment classes called *traditional investments*.

Let's briefly look at each type of traditional investment. A *stock* is a type of investment that represents an ownership share in a company. Investors buy stocks that they think are likely to increase in value over time and perhaps provide income by paying dividends. A *bond* represents a loan funded by an investor to a borrower, such as a corporation or government. Investors buy bonds because most bonds offer a predictable income stream. Also, by holding the bonds until maturity, they get back the entire principal. Thus, bonds provide a way to preserve capital while investing.

Cash equivalents are short-term securities, which have high credit quality and are highly liquid. Examples of cash equivalents include certificates of deposit, money market funds, and Treasury bills. Still, these cash equivalents may not even keep up with inflation. *The Savvy Investor's Guide to Building Wealth Through Traditional Investments* discusses investing in stocks, bonds, and cash equivalents.

Instead of investing in individual stocks and bonds, many individuals invest in pooled investment vehicles (PIVs) through their retirement plans. PIVs are investment funds that commingle many different investors' monies to buy portfolios that reflect specific investment objectives. PIVs offer such advantages as professional management, diversification, government regulation, low initial investment, and liquidity. They can also involve high costs, including management and performance fees and a lack of choice and control over the fund's assets. *The Savvy Investor's Guide to Pooled Investments* focuses on five popular PIVs: open-end funds, more commonly called mutual funds, closed-end funds, exchange-traded funds (ETFs), unit investment trusts, and real estate investment trusts.

If you're new to investing, traditional investments are a great place to start building your portfolio and planning for retirement because of their many advantages. Although cash and bonds are relatively safe investments, the stock market can be risky and subject to considerable volatility. Of course, you can lose money if a stock's market price declines, but you can also lose money if you sell a bond before its maturity date for less than what you paid for it or if the issuer defaults on its payments.

Although most investors are generally satisfied with portfolios consisting of traditional investments, others may want their portfolios to include other investment opportunities.

A whole world of investment options awaits you that extends beyond stocks and bonds. Any financial asset that falls outside traditional investment categories is an *alternative investment*. In practice, the lines between traditional and alternative investments are not universal.

Alternative investments can either be public or private investments. Previously, some of these alternative investments and their associated strategies were only available to institutional and high-net-worth investors. Today, more retail investors have access to alternative investments or other investment vehicles that employ techniques previously confined to alternative investments. However, just because such vehicles exist doesn't necessarily mean that they're right for you. Although alternative investments are often inappropriate for smaller portfolios, they often play a role in more sizable portfolios. Generally speaking, retail investors should allocate only a small percentage (5%–15%) to such investments.

The core alternative investments are hedge funds and private equity, primarily venture capital and buyout funds. Although these alternative investments are unavailable to all investors, they have historically played a critical role in the industry's evolution. Additionally, these categories accounted for much of the capital allocated to alternative investments. Tangible alternative investments consist of real estate, commodities, infrastructure, and collectibles. Each category of alternative investments has a distinct set of attributes. For example, alternative investments differ from traditional investments due to their higher fees and different legal structures. However, not all real assets are tangible such as patents and copyrights. Introduction Fig. 1 shows various categories of traditional and alternative investments.

Traditional Investments
- Stocks
- Bonds
- Cash

Tangible Alternative Investments
- Real estate
- Commodities
- Infrastructure
- Collectibles

} Widely used and available to all investors

Core Alternative Investments
- Hedge funds
- Private equity

} Selectively used and only available to accredited investors

Introduction Figure 1. Types of Traditional and Alternative Investments

Source: Adapted from World Economic Forum. Retrieved from http://www3.weforum.org/docs/WEF_Alternative_Investments_2020_An_Introduction_to_AI.pdf

Here's a brief overview of each alternative investment category.

- Core alternative investments

  o *Hedge funds.* A *hedge fund* is typically a limited partnership that uses various strategies and tactics to invest its clients' money to generate investment gains or provide a hedge against unforeseen market changes. Hedge fund managers invest in numerous financial instruments such as stocks, bonds, complex derivatives, options, commodities, and other esoteric investments. Although a hedge fund's initial intent was to protect investment portfolios from market uncertainty (thus the name "hedge") while generating positive returns in both up and down markets, most hedge funds don't hedge risk. Hedge funds cater to investors with ultra-deep pockets. Although the lowest minimum investment starts at $100,000, most require at least $1,000,000. Thus, for most individual investors, these amounts are hardly spare change.

o *Private equity.* *Private equity* is a generic term referring to the funds used by investors to invest in private companies (i.e., firms not publicly-traded on a stock exchange) or to engage in buyouts of publicly-traded firms with the intent of taking them private. Two major types of private equity are venture capital and buyout (leveraged buyout). *Venture capital* refers to an investment in small, early-stage to growth-stage companies without obtaining majority control. Investors can directly invest in start-ups and private companies or use venture capital funds. A *buyout* or *leveraged buyout* is a financial transaction that involves buying a controlling interest of an existing or mature firm, often using high levels of debt to finance the acquisition, and then taking the company private. As a private entity, owners structure the company intending to sell it in the future at an anticipated profit. Using a substantial amount of debt enables the acquirer to increase potential returns by leveraging the seller's assets.

• Tangible alternative investments

o *Real estate.* Real Estate investing involves the purchase, ownership, management, rental, or sale of real estate to earn a profit. The four major categories of real estate are residential, commercial, industrial, and land. Investors may hold such investments in various structures, including individual properties, limited partnerships, private and publicly-traded securities backed by pools of properties or mortgages, and real estate backed loans.

o *Commodities*. *Commodities* typically refer to physical (hard) assets used in production, such as agricultural products, energy, and metals. Commodities don't generate cash flows and often involve storage, transportation, and insurance costs not found in other assets. However, the Commodity Futures Trading Commission decided that virtual currencies such as bitcoins could also be considered commodities.

o *Infrastructure*. *Infrastructure* refers to long-lived assets that provide basic structures and facilities needed to operate a society or enterprise, such as transportation, communication, sewage, water, and electric systems. Although infrastructure is often built or managed by governments and funded publicly, infrastructure can also be financed privately or through public–private partnerships.

o *Collectibles*. A *collectible* is an item that can be worth more than its original selling price because of its rarity or popularity. Thus, collectibles are physical goods that have value only because of a widely shared emotional or societal attachment. Examples of items in this asset class include art, antiques, wine, jewelry, rare coins, vintage or exotic cars, and baseball cards.

> *"Remember, people don't invest in collectibles, they spend money on them."*
> Andrew Beattie

Although collectibles may sound more fun and interesting than other types of investments, this book excludes them. Why? Collectibles are less illiquid than traditional securities, and owners don't receive income from collectibles. Some collectibles can be costly. You can also lose money if the collectible is damaged or demand wanes. More importantly, you won't necessarily make a good return. Overall, collectibles have lower returns than a money market account, most bond funds, and stock market index fund. Although investing in collectibles adds diversification to your portfolio, perhaps the primary reason for buying collectibles is that you enjoy owning them beyond the potential return you may receive from selling them. Some people are passionate about collectibles and enjoy gaining the required specialized skill and knowledge to succeed in this volatile market segment. Otherwise, you could get burned if you don't know what you're doing in a specific marketplace. You should also be aware that this market is teaming with conmen. Thus, if you think you can invest in collectibles the same way you invest in stocks or bonds, you'll likely encounter some unexpected challenges. Without being a real expert, you unlikely to experience any return on your investment. From an investment perspective, the bottom line is that collectibles' unique risks often outweigh the financial rewards.

Many other alternative investments are available to investors beyond the five major types discussed in this book. For example, investment banks create structured products by combining two or more assets, and sometimes multiple asset classes, that payout based on those underlying assets' performance. Structured products include different types of collateralized debt obligations and other derivatives. These alternative investments, including more exotic alternative investments, are beyond the scope of this book.

Before investing, you should understand the differences between traditional and alternative investments. Compared with traditional investments, alternative investments tend to be less liquid, more opaque, more challenging to value, and offer investors limited access to information. Because alternative investments are subject to less regulation, potential investors face a greater risk of investment scams and fraud if they don't perform sufficient *due diligence*, which means exercising reasonable care before buying or making an investment. Some alternative investments, such as hedge funds and private equity, also have limited and possibly biased historical returns data. Another problem is that measuring historical risk and benchmarking can be problematic. Additionally, alternative investments involve higher fees and have more restrictions on redemptions and unique tax considerations. Further, managers tend to be highly specialized and hold relatively more concentrated portfolios.

For some alternative investments, such as hedge funds and private equity funds, only accredited investors can invest directly in the assets and are out of reach of most individual investors. An *accredited investor* is a person or a business entity who is permitted to invest in non-registered securities. Accredited investors have more than $1 million of assets (excluding their primary residence) or an annual income of more than $200,000 ($300,000 if married) to invest in non-public companies. Thus, those primarily engaging in such alternative investments are high-net-worth or sophisticated individuals, registered brokers, investment advisors, and institutions such as pension funds, sovereign wealth funds, banks, insurance companies, foundations, and endowments.

Despite their drawbacks, some can make a strong case for including alternative investments in a portfolio. The primary reason investors add

> *"Building wealth is a marathon not a sprint. Discipline is the key ingredient."*
> Dave Ramsey

them to their portfolios is for the potential of enhanced risk-adjusted performance, consisting of high returns, lower risk, or a combination of the two. Why? For example, when stocks or bonds underperform, a hedge fund or private equity firm may cushion the blow over the long term with higher returns. Additionally, the correlation between traditional and alternative asset classes' returns is often low, which reduces overall portfolio risk. However, because the correlations vary across time and between categories of alternative investments, you might not realize much in the way of diversification benefits. For example, during periods of financial crisis, the correlation and volatility of returns increase, reducing diversification benefits. In other instances, these investments offer inflation-hedging benefits, especially commodities and real estate. Introduction Figure 2 provides a general overview of some pros and cons of investing in alternative investments relative to traditional investments.

The traditional, diversified strategies that worked in the past may no longer be as profitable as investors become more sophisticated. Alternative investments represent a

> *"Before you invest in something, invest the time to understand it."*
> Robert T. Kiyosaki

Pros
- Diversification potential
- High returns with due diligence
- Inflation hedge
- New exposures and opportunities
- Cusion market volatility
- Tax benefits

Cons
- Less liquid, regulated, and transparent for private investments
- More difficult to value
- More complex fee structures
- Higher minimum requirements and potential risks

Introduction Figure 2. Pros and Cons of Alternative Investments Relative to Traditional Investments

universe unto themselves. Over the past several decades, the alternative investments' industry has become a crucial component of the global financial system and world economy. Some alternative investments are now more accessible to non-accredited retail investors, not just high-net-worth individuals and institutional investors. The reason is the emergence of alternative mutual funds and ETFs, also known as alt funds or liquid alternative investments. Since alt funds trade publicly, they are subject to registration with the Securities and Exchange Commission (SEC) and regulation, specifically by the Investment Company Act of 1940.

The purpose of *The Savvy Investor's Guide to Building Wealth Through Alternative Investments* is to help you understand what you're getting into with alternative investments if you decide to invest in them. Although many other alternative investments are available, this book focuses on five primary types: hedge funds, private equity, real estate, commodities, and infrastructure. This book uses plain English to explain concepts and terms that are often puzzling to investors. It attempts to remove some of the mystery surrounding alternative investments so that you can determine whether any of these investments are right for you. However, investing in alternative investments requires a certain amount of knowledge and expertise to improve the likelihood of success. You need to evaluate each alternative investment based on its own merits and your situation. If you're willing to gain that proficiency, then you may be able to build long-term wealth by taking advantage of the benefits that each type of investment has to offer. Otherwise, investing in alternative investments can be a complicated and risky bet and should be avoided.

1

HEDGE FUNDS: INVESTING FOR SHORTER-TERM OPPORTUNITIES

"Many hedge fund managers have become billionaires; perhaps this – plus their reputations as the smartest guys in the room – is why they have captured the investing public's imagination."

Barry Ritholtz, Chief Investment
Officer of Ritholtz Wealth Management LLC

Much controversy surrounds hedge funds. In the aftermath of the financial crisis of 2007–2008, many politicians and commentators identified the hedge fund industrys a major cause of this financial crisis. The real reasons are much more complicated. Although hedge funds are convenient targets, they shouldn't be the center of the controversy. Ordinary investors typically have little understanding of hedge funds and with good reason. Hedge funds are generally private,

"Private-equity and hedge-fund guys typically come into a situation of mediocrity, where rapid change may result in a profit."
Austin Ligon

discreet, opaque, unregulated, and require large buy-ins. The purpose of this chapter is to help you determine whether hedge funds are appropriate for your investment portfolio.

A major misconception about hedge funds is that they're relatively new. Alfred Winslow Jones launched the first hedge fund in 1949 through his company A. W. Jones & Company. Jones wrote an article for *Fortune* in 1948 about current investment trends. He discussed how he took $40,000 of his own money along with $60,000 from other investors and created a fund that sold certain stocks short to minimize the risk of the long-term stock positions he held. This strategy later became known as long/short investing. *Short selling* is borrowing someone else's securities, selling them, and then hopefully repurchasing them at a lower price and returning the borrowed shares to the original owner. Thus, short sellers are motivated by the belief that a security's price is likely to decline ("what goes up must come down"), enabling them to repurchase shares at a lower price to make a profit. Jones also used leverage to magnify returns. *Leverage* involves using borrowed funds for an investment expecting that the investment returns exceed the interest paid on the borrowed funds.

In 1952, Jones converted his fund to a limited partnership creating a compensation structure for the fund manager, a general partner (GP), which included a 20% incentive fee based on performance. A *limited partnership* is a legal structure, in which limited partners provide capital for investment and the GP controls. Many limited partnerships are set up so that you can only lose the amount invested. This new structure ushered in the modern hedge fund.

Hedge funds continued to gain traction into the mid-1960s, at which point another article in *Fortune* highlighted their superior performance relative to mutual funds resulting in further demand. Hedge fund strategies were evolving and splintering. Jones's original vision of hedge funds "hedging" risk gave way to other riskier strategies. In the late 1960s and early 1970s, heavy losses mounted for these new strategies, and hedge fund growth remained dormant until the mid-1980s. In 1986, an *Institutional Investor* article highlighting the Tiger Fund, with its double-digit performance, ignited growth. Hedge fund strategies, discussed later in this chapter, continued to evolve and expand as fund managers incorporated derivatives. *Derivatives* are securities that derive their value from another security or reference, such as interest rates. Some use derivatives to speculate on movements in the value of an underlying security without taking ownership.

Growth continued until around the turn of the twenty-first century, with many hedge fund failures occurring. Growth reignited with the number of hedge funds growing from about 2,000 in 2002 to around 16,000 by the end of 2019. According to Preqin, the United States remains a crucial driver of the global hedge fund industry, accounting for 75% of the approximate $3.61 trillion in global assets as of November 2019. Preqin provides data and information on private capital and hedge funds, including market-wide benchmarks.

The more recent hedge fund growth is attributable to several factors such as the low correlations between hedge fund returns and traditional assets, including stocks and bonds. Low correlation among asset returns creates greater diversification and the ability to take advantage of both ownership (long positions) and short positions, and strategies that can produce high returns in a low-yield environment. Since the financial crisis of 2007–2008, growth has mainly occurred with larger funds, which investors perceive as having better risk management systems in place. Hedge funds provide savvy investors with potentially attractive shorter-term investing opportunities.

1.1. WHAT IS A HEDGE FUND, AND
HOW DOES IT WORK?

A *hedge fund* is a fancy name for an investment partnership that pools capital from individuals or institutional investors and invests this capital in various assets using alternative and complex strategies and techniques. The initial intent of hedge funds was to allow larger investors to "hedge their bets" by diversifying into different asset classes. As private firms, hedge funds are subject to little regulation. Their managers are compensated based on assets under management (AUM) and performance-related incentive fees. They can use leverage, derivatives, and short positions, often associated with complex investment strategies. Hedge funds are only available to *accredited* or *qualified investors*, including individuals who have an annual income over $200,000 ($300,000 if married) for the past two years or net worth of more than $1 million and institutional investors such as endowments and pension funds. These rules, mandated by the Securities and Exchange Commission (SEC), assume that qualified investors understand hedge funds' potential risks. In 2016, new rules increased the investor pool by allowing registered brokers, investment advisors, and individual investors to show relevant educational or job experience with unregistered securities to buy hedge funds.

1.2. HOW DOES A HEDGE FUND DIFFER
FROM A MUTUAL FUND?

Both hedge funds and mutual funds are PIVs. A PIV is an investment fund created by pooling investments from many investors. However, several features distinguish hedge funds from mutual funds. Worldwide, as of

October 2019, 9,599 mutual funds controlled more than $17.71 trillion of assets. In contrast, hedge funds had holdings of about $3.61 trillion. Both use professional money managers and diversify their holdings. Beyond sheer size, several other features differentiate these two PIVs.

- *Investment strategies.* Mutual funds are readily available to the public for investment and include traditional investments such as stocks, bonds, and cash. Some mutual fund strategies involve taking a short position or using leverage. In contrast, hedge funds are harder to classify. They may carry considerably more risk, employ leverage, engage in hedging strategies, or pursue arbitrage opportunities. *Arbitrage* is the practice of taking advantage of a price difference between two or more markets. Hedge funds also have fewer investing constraints than mutual funds and hence have greater flexibility.

- *Regulation.* In the United States, the Securities Act of 1933, Securities Exchange Act of 1934, the Investment Company Act of 1940, and the Investment Advisers Act of 1940 regulate mutual funds. However, the Investment Company Act provides the most specific guidance related to structure, operations, and pricing. Before the financial crisis of 2007–2008, hedge funds avoided most of the regulatory requirements that mutual funds had to follow. The Dodd-Frank Wall Street Reform and Consumer Protection Act of 2010 (Dodd-Frank) required larger hedge funds to register with the SEC.

- *Clientele.* Few restrictions exist on mutual fund investors other than perhaps a minimum investment level. As

> *"Hedge fund managers charge so much more than mutual fund managers; alpha is even harder to come by. They end up selling a variety of things beyond mere outperformance."*
>
> Barry Ritholtz

previously noted, only accredited investors can invest in hedge funds. Loosening of the restrictions occurred in 2016 to include some financial professionals and those who can successfully document that their educational and training background permits them to understand hedge fund strategies' more complex nature.

- *Fee structure.* Mutual fund investors are subject to management fees, possible sales charges, and other fees. Hedge fund investors pay both a management fee based on AUM and an incentive (performance) fee based on a manager exceeding a pre-determined benchmark return.

- *Liquidity.* Compared to mutual funds, hedge funds are less liquid because you can't withdraw from your investment any time you want. Some hedge funds establish *gates* that allow limited time windows to exchange shares or impose *lock-up periods* that restrict investors from redeeming their funds for up to two years.

- *Transparency.* Mutual funds provide greater transparency to investors about their holdings and strategies. Hedge funds tend to disclose less information to their investors to guard their superior strategies. Their secrecy stems from a fear that other managers may replicate successful strategies, reducing return potential.

- *Self-investment.* In a hedge fund, the expectation is that the manager invests in the fund. In contrast, the manager of a mutual fund doesn't face the same expectation.

1.3. WHAT ARE THE DIFFERENT APPROACHES FOR OWNING A HEDGE FUND?

Three approaches are available to access ownership to hedge funds.

- *Direct approach*. The direct approach involves investing in individual hedge funds. You can select this method if you're an accredited investor or meet revised requirements regarding career or education and experience.

> *"Successful hedge funds will be entrepreneurial; it is the essence of the craft."*
>   Paul Singer

  The direct approach allows you to conduct your due diligence into fund selection. *Due diligence* involves performing an in-depth analysis of financial, legal, and operational information on a fund before investing capital. Examples of the biggest hedge funds in the United States include Bridgewater Associates, Renaissance Technologies, and AQR Capital Management.

- *Fund of hedge funds approach*. A *fund of hedge funds* (FOF) is a hedge fund that invests in a portfolio of other hedge funds. The FOF manager makes decisions about strategy and fund selection, portfolio construction and composition, and risk management and monitoring. This approach ensures better diversification, because it includes multiple funds. If you select this method, you don't have direct control of selected funds and have two layers of fees. Each fund in a FOF is eligible for AUM and incentive fees, as is the FOF manager. An example of a FOF is the Blackstone Alternative Asset Management (BAAM) Fund.

- *Indexed approach*. You can also select index funds that try to mimic the underlying strategy of a given hedge fund. An example of this strategy is a replication product.

Managers try to identify the key measures that drive hedge fund performance and replicate the exposures through publicly traded securities. ProShares Hedge Replication is an example of a replication product.

1.4. WHY ARE HEDGE FUNDS VITAL TO THE FINANCIAL INDUSTRY AND SOCIETY IN GENERAL?

Hedge funds comprise a relatively small fraction of the global capital markets, and individual investors have limited abilities to invest in hedge funds directly. Given this situation, what makes hedge funds so crucial to investors?

- *Use of derivatives.* Since many hedge fund strategies use derivatives, implicit leverage causes hedge funds to have a disproportionally larger influence in the financial markets. The leverage occurs because derivative contracts only require a relatively small investment called the *margin* to control a considerably larger contract value. For instance, if the margin requirement for a derivatives contract is 5%, then the contract has $1/0.05 = 20$ times leveraging component.

- *Indirect investment.* Although restrictions limit individual investors' ability to invest in hedge funds directly, these investors may indirectly participate in hedge funds through institutional investors such as pension funds, endowment funds, insurance companies, central banks, and FOFs. In fact, institutional investors are the primary investors in hedge funds. Therefore, hedge funds can have a disproportionate economic impact as events occurring in the hedge fund industry can trickle down to other critical areas within the financial markets.

- *Liquidity providers.* Hedge funds provide a source of liquidity funding in the market, particularly during a financial crisis. Hedge funds played an essential role in mitigating the liquidity crisis that emerged in 2008 due to the 2007–2008 financial crisis.

- *Less regulation.* Due to the lighter regulatory burden that hedge funds bear compared to traditional investment options, these funds provide an opportunity to test new strategies and innovations in asset allocation, trading, and portfolio management. Many individuals with highly analytical educational backgrounds manage hedge funds.

- *Foreshadowing changes in market dynamics.* Because their strategies tend to be more cutting edge, hedge funds provide the first tangible warning signs of a larger systemic impending problem. For example, because of their flexibility with short positions, a long/short hedge fund manager may reduce the net systematic risk exposure in anticipation of a market decline. *Systematic risk* is the risk inherent to the entire market that diversification can't eliminate. Additionally, hedge funds engaging in activist investing have become an essential and effective tool for corporate governance.

1.5. WHAT ADVANTAGES DO HEDGE FUNDS OFFER INVESTORS?

Here are some advantages that hedge fund exposure brings to a portfolio.

- *Alternative investment strategies.* Many of these strategies can offer higher returns but carry greater risks associated with their aggressive nature. Strategies may include investments in international financial markets, leverage, derivatives, and a long/short strategy. Such strategies can enhance returns but also increase the chance of huge losses.

Using risk management tools is often necessary to control risk within the portfolio.

- *Return enhancement.* Due to the nature of many of these strategies, hedge funds can target high return opportunities with some strategies reducing overall risk because of low correlation with traditional investments. Targeted global opportunities allow for harvesting gains through evaluating investment opportunities and forecasting.

- *Diversification.* Because many of the strategies pursued by hedge funds have risks that differ from traditional investments, hedge funds can offer diversification benefits to reduce a portfolio's overall risk level. Lowering overall portfolio risk reduces the probability of extreme losses.

- *Expert management.* By offering incentive fees based on performance, hedge funds increase competition among managers. Consequently, hedge funds attract some of the brightest minds in the industry. Such managers may develop investment strategies that produce results that outpace those available in the public markets.

> *"I don't think that hedge funds are bad per se. I think they're just one more financial tool. And in that sense, they're useful."*
>
> Barack Obama

1.6. WHAT ARE THE DISADVANTAGES OR DRAWBACKS OF OWNING HEDGE FUNDS?

Hedge fund advocates often paint a colorful picture but neglect to discuss any negative aspects. Hedge fund investing isn't for everyone. Here are some areas that represent short-comings when considering investing in hedge funds.

- *Investment fees.* Although incentive fees, also called *carried interest* or *carry*, may attract top talent, such costs represent a substantial expense for hedge fund investors. *Carried interest* is a share of any profits that the GPs (fund managers) of hedge funds receive as compensation. Historically, investment fees included a 2% AUM fee and a 20% incentive fee based on exceeding a pre-determined return threshold such as 8%. These fees decreased after the financial crisis of 2007–2008, mainly due to poor hedge fund performance and competition but remain high compared to mutual funds. Although incentive fees may motivate the fund manager to improve fund performance, they may also encourage excessive risk-taking behavior.

> *"Perhaps the best news is that hedge fund returns are not highly correlated with those of traditional portfolios, suggesting that this asset class may bring a substantial and enduring diversification benefit."*
> David M. Smith

- *Measuring risk.* Hedge fund returns don't follow the same risk patterns as more traditional investments. Instead of return distributions that follow more predictable patterns, hedge funds often have a return profile that can include huge gains or losses. Investors refer to this pattern as *fat tails*, which result in higher probabilities of enormous gains or losses than would be expected with stocks and bonds.

- *Leverage.* Many hedge fund strategies employ leverage, which magnifies returns. In a market downturn, for example, leverage can increase losses. To meet loan repayments, hedge fund managers may have to sell investments at a low price, eventually leading to financial distress, including possible liquidation.

- *Lock-up periods*. Hedge funds often have lock-up periods that limit the withdrawal of funds. For instance, some hedge funds only allow withdrawing funds on a quarterly, semi-annual, or annual basis.

- *Lack of transparency*. Because hedge funds have fewer reporting requirements than other PIVs, such as mutual funds, the strategies often seem secretive. To their credit, hedge fund managers don't want to reveal successful trading strategies and positions to competitors. However, without knowledge of investment strategies, you're vulnerable to selecting a fund inconsistent with your investment philosophy.

1.7. WHAT ARE THE MAJOR CATEGORIES AND SUBCATEGORIES OF HEDGE FUNDS?

Due to the array of investment strategies, no uniform classification system is available for hedge funds. Different experts group hedge funds in various configurations based on broad themes that emerge across funds. For purposes of this chapter, hedge funds consist of four major categories: (1) global macro and managed futures funds, (2) event-driven hedge funds, (3) relative value (arbitrage) funds, and (4) equity funds.

- *Global macro and managed futures funds*. Characteristics of the first group are its broad mandates and the presence of both discretionary and systematic traders. Discretionary traders use a subjective, more opinion-based means of decision-making.

A discretionary trader may set up entry and exit points for an investment based on emotions. For example, the trader could establish entry and exit points based on a percentage change in an underlying security price. Systematic traders use fixed rules to determine entry and exit points that they can program into a computer.

> *"The number-one job of the hedge-fund manager is not to make sure that you can retire with a smile on your face - it's for him to retire with a smile on his face."*
>
> Mark Cuban

o *Global macro strategies* tend to be opportunistic, top-down in nature, focusing on global events. In other words, these strategies seek opportunities wherever they arise that are driven by macroeconomic forecasts. Global macro strategies focus on exploiting opportunities related to currencies, interest rates, and stock indices. The main risks relate to market (systematic) risk, event risk, and leverage. Because these strategies focus on macroeconomic assessment, market risk becomes a concern if their forecasts are wrong. Event risk can run the gamut from an unexpected failure of an international trade deal to a weather disaster. Leverage can magnify both gains and losses. These strategies have done well in volatile market conditions, including the financial crisis of 2007–2008. Examples of the largest global macro hedge funds are Bridgewater Associates, Caxton Associates, and Soros Fund Management.

o *Managed futures strategies* use active trading of futures and forward contracts on commodities, financial assets, and foreign currencies. These strategies focus more on systematic trading using technical analysis. *Systematic* or *mechanical trading* is a way of defining trade goals, risk controls, and rules that can methodically make investment and trading decisions. *Technical analysis* focuses on identifying patterns of prices or volume to discern entry and exit points. The most significant risks for these strategies are a lack of understanding (transparency) of the strategies employed, invalid models, excess capacity for narrow trading strategies, regulatory changes, and a lack of volatility in the pricing of futures contracts. An example of a managed futures hedge fund is Abbey Capital Futures Strategies.

- *Event-driven hedge funds.* This group of hedge fund strategies attempts to take advantage of pricing inefficiencies due to uncertainty about corporate events.

  o *Activist strategies* attempt to identify corporations where leadership is not currently maximizing shareholder wealth, which creates opportunities to influence the corporate governance structure positively. *Corporate governance* is the system of rules and practices for operating a firm.

  > "Hedge funds are a very efficient way of managing money. But there are clearly some risks. Hedge funds use credit and credit is a source of instability. Transactions involving credit should be regulated."
  >
  > George Soros

  Several categories of activists exist. Financial activists focus on increasing stock prices, while social activists try to change corporate investments and structures to benefit society. Some activists work with management to improve conditions, whereas others threaten management with adverse consequences such as dismissal. Some are more active, establishing positions to augment their voice, while others are more passive. Activist strategies often target excessive management compensation and ineffective board oversight, and inappropriate company financing choices and dividend policies. The principal risk of activist strategies is associated with a lack of effectiveness in generating change within the organization they target. Atlantic Investment Group is an example of an activist strategy hedge fund.

o *Merger arbitrage strategies* seek to exploit opportunities that exist from a potential merger. These strategies use leverage to buy the target firm's stock, and short sell the acquiring firm's stock. The logic is that the price for a target firm often increases as the acquiring firm, seeking to attract target shareholders, offers a considerable premium above the target's current stock price. Furthermore, a bidding contest for a target firm among suitors benefits target shareholders. The prime risk of merger arbitrage is the possibility that bidders may abandon a proposed deal, which often causes a decline in the target's stock price. Of course, hedge fund managers may implement the opposite strategy if they feel the proposed deal is likely to fall through. Additional risks of merger arbitrage include governmental actions to block a merger or the acquiring firm's inability to secure financing for the merger. The Gabelli ABC Fund is an example of a merger arbitrage hedge fund.

o *Distressed debt strategies* assume many forms. They may include taking short positions on firms expected to be liquidated, buying undervalued securities that are likely to survive and thrive, or identifying ways to enhance firm value due to reorganization, often through court action.

Aurelius Capital Management is an example of a hedge fund using such strategies.

- *Relative value strategies.* These strategies focus on exploiting relative mispricing between security offerings within the same company or similar securities. The strategies take a long position on the security the manager considers underpriced and a short position on the security the manager views as overpriced to exploit price discrepancies as prices revert and return to equilibrium. Managers often identify mispricing by looking at deviations from historical pricing relations. The main risk associated with these strategies is that mispricing may not converge or may even widen.

  o *Convertible bond arbitrage* strategies target *convertible bonds*, which are securities that give bondholders the right to exchange their bonds for the firm's common stock. The strategy involves taking a long position in the convertible bond and simultaneously taking a short position in the company's stock. The objective is to benefit from the option component's mispricing to convert from a bond to a stock. This strategy tries to eliminate equity exposure while still receiving coupon payments on the bonds by shorting the stock. Critical concerns for these strategies involve interest rate risk, equity price and volatility changes, illiquid positions, and financial crises. *Interest rate risk* is the risk associated with a decline in a bond's value caused by an increase in interest rates. Thus, interest rate risk is the risk borne by bond owners from fluctuating interest rates. Whitebox Relative Value Partners is an example of a convertible bond arbitrage fund.

o *Volatility arbitrage strategies* try to capitalize on differences in implied volatility between two securities, often based on options. *Implied volatility* is the estimated volatility embedded into the option contract's price. An *option* gives the buyer the right to buy or sell an asset at a specific price over a finite period. For a company with many option contracts trading in the market, the implied volatility – what's "priced" into option prices – should be identical. A higher volatility means higher option prices, because it increases the likelihood for greater stock movement, making the option more valuable. The strategy involves buying options that have lower implied volatility and selling options that have higher implied volatility. A profit results if the market eventually corrects the inconsistency in volatility assessments before the options expire. The risk of these strategies mainly comes from a lack of convergence of volatility between the two options. One example of a volatility arbitrage hedge fund is Blue Diamond Non-Directional Strategy.

o *Fixed-income arbitrage strategies* try to profit from small pricing discrepancies between two similar fixed income securities, buying the security that is considered inexpensive and shorting the more expensive one. As pricing discrepancies are small, these strategies often are highly leveraged. Variations include spread strategies focusing on two bonds of similar maturity and yield curve strategies concentrating on different maturities. Once again, the main risk is that prices don't converge as anticipated. Bond defaults, liquidity crises, and interest rate risk are additional risks. Asgard Fixed Income I Ltd is representative of a fixed income arbitrage hedge fund.

- *Equity hedge funds* try to align portfolio exposures to market risk while identifying mispriced securities. The chief concern is incorrectly analyzing the optimal level of systematic risk exposure or misidentifying opportunities for mispriced securities.

  o *Long-short funds* form portfolios of securities held (long positions) and securities sold short to calibrate to an acceptable level of systematic risk. Net positions can range from positions holding systematic risk greater than that of the overall market to positions that move in the opposite direction. Pelham Long/Short Small Cap Ltd Class A is an example of a long-short hedge fund.

  o *Market neutral strategies* attempt to eliminate systematic risk by offsetting the risk of long positions with the risk of short positions creating a portfolio unaffected by market risk. *Long positions* are those securities that analysts consider undervalued, and *short positions* are deemed overvalued. Thus, the profit potential relates to exploiting long and short positions. Hedge fund managers use substantial leverage to magnify returns. Covalis Capital Master Class A is an example of a market-neutral hedge fund.

  o *Short selling strategies* try to take advantage of market declines by initiating short positions that benefit from a drop in a security's price. An example of a short-selling hedge fund is Greenlight Capital.

1.8. HOW ARE HEDGE FUNDS REGULATED?

Hedge fund regulation varies based on each country. In the United States, the Investment Company Act of 1940 exempted hedge funds from the regulatory oversight associated with mutual funds (registration with the SEC) by allowing only accredited investors or qualified purchasers to access hedge funds. As a result of the financial crisis of 2007–2008, Congress enacted Dodd-Frank. This Act requires registration for hedge fund managers with AUM: (1) between $25 million and $100 million whose primary business is in a state that doesn't require registration of investment advisors, (2) above $100 million and maintains managed accounts, or (3) above $150 million and doesn't maintain managed accounts. A *managed account* is an investment account owned by an individual investor and overseen by a hired professional money manager. Overseas hedge funds must also register with the SEC if they have more than 15 US-based clients and AUM above $25 million. Registered hedge funds must appoint a chief compliance officer (CCO) to create a compliance culture that includes sufficient resources, support, and authority. The CCO is responsible for compliance procedures testing and reporting, reviewing market materials, recordkeeping, annually reviewing policies and compliance issues, and developing a code of ethics.

In Europe, the Alternative Investment Fund Manager Directive regulated hedge funds. Hedge funds register in their home country, with approval granting a marketing passport across the European Union. Granting the passport requires fund managers to meet minimum capital requirements, have professional indemnity insurance, and conduct stress testing and liquidity monitoring. It also requires managers to adhere to leverage limits, meet guidelines for profit reporting, identify compensation policy, demonstrate minimum experience and reputation, identify valuation methods, and meet guidelines for reporting profits.

Regulation in Asia is more fragmented based on the country. For instance, in Hong Kong, the Securities and Futures Commission regulates hedge funds. It requires transparency, a minimum AUM of $100 million, five years of management experience by at least two personnel, and documented due diligence on investors. In Singapore, the Monetary Authority of Singapore regulates hedge funds with similar experience requirements as Hong Kong, a minimum subscription of SGD 100,000, and documenting the minimum risk management standards. In South Korea, the Financial Supervisory Service regulates hedge funds and requires licensing and minimum experience requirements. Hedge funds must show adequate controls and meet a minimum size threshold. In Japan, the Securities and Exchange Surveillance Commission prevents hedge funds from investing offshore and requires minimum disclosure and licensing with adequate controls demonstrated.

1.9. HOW ARE HEDGE FUNDS TAXED?

Hedge funds are structured as either limited partnerships or limited liability companies (LLCs). Both structures are taxed as a partnership, making them *pass-through vehicles*, which means no taxation occurs at the fund level. Instead, income is "passed through" to investors who report returns on their individual tax returns. As such, investment strategy may affect tax rates. For instance, the government taxes long-term capital gains generated by hedge funds at a long-term capital gains rate.

1.10. WHAT SELECTION CRITERIA SHOULD INVESTORS USE TO EVALUATE HEDGE FUNDS?

You should carefully consider several criteria when determining if a hedge fund is an appropriate investment vehicle or selecting a fund.

- *Investment philosophy*. Before selecting a hedge fund, you should understand its nature – what type of assets it holds and the parameters under which it operates. Although gaining access to the manager for a conversation would be helpful, reviewing updates and quarterly reports can provide valuable information about the fund. You shouldn't expect the manager to disclose current positions that could reveal the fund's strategies and potentially damage its success. However, you should be able to get general information about the fund's overall strategy. The inability to gain information on how the fund operates is a major red flag to avoid investing in it. Understanding a specific hedge fund's risk-return trade-offs is essential to ensuring an appropriate investment for your portfolio.

- *Risk exposure.* You can usually deduce a fund's risk exposure by studying its *offering memorandum* or *document*, a disclosure document provided to investors for their investment consideration. An offering memorandum operates in the same way as a prospectus for stock offerings. It contains various features and sections such as an offering's terms, investor suitability, risk factors, management team, use of proceeds, and tax implications. In general, either through the offering memorandum or other research, you should be able to identify some basic risk measures. To what extent does the fund use leverage? Does a holding or strategy exceed a desirable exposure level? Has the manager followed the fund's stated strategy? How is trading activity monitored and audited?

- *Manager reputation.* What information can you ascertain about the manager's background, including past performance? Does the manager hold key certifications or designations relevant to the position? Is the manager registered with the SEC or another appropriate regulatory body? Are any civil or criminal actions pending or

---

executed against the manager? Pending actions don't imply guilt but could mean that the manager may be distracted in performing requisite duties. The bottom line is that you should be satisfied with the qualifications of your hedge fund manager. Here are some websites that may help you find more information about hedge fund managers.

o Form ADV. The advisor's registration form, which details disciplinary history within the securities industry, is located on the SEC's Investment Adviser Public Disclosure (IAPD) website (http://www.adviserinfo.sec.gov/iapd/content/iapdmain/iapd_sitemap.aspx).

o If the advisor doesn't appear on the website, you can check the state securities regulator (http://www.nasaa.org/about-us/contact-us/contact-your-regulator/) or FINRA's BrokerCheck database (http://www.finra.org/investors/toolscalculators/brokercheck/).

• *External support.* The manager's broker is likely to be aware of the fund's investing philosophy. Outside accounting firms understand fund dynamics. Outside counsel may know of vulnerabilities facing the manager. The manager should make these individuals available to you or your representative. The key is that others outside of the manager's influence handle these functions. You should be aware of funds internally handling these functions may lack necessary checks and balances.

> *"The risks facing hedge funds are non-linear and more complex than those facing traditional asset classes. Such risks are currently not widely appreciated or well-understood."*
>
> Andrew Lo

- *Past performance.* Although past performance isn't a guarantee of future returns, some evidence exists of return persistence for individual hedge fund managers. Also, examining past performance may offer additional insights into the fund's investment philosophy. How does the manager's performance compare to others claiming a similar philosophy over different economic cycle phases? Identifying patterns may help you better understand the conditions under which a manager could do well. Because some hedge fund holdings are illiquid and don't have a readily available market value, you should understand how to value such assets.

- *Limits on redemption.* Most hedge funds restrict your ability to redeem shares. Some funds limit redemptions to four or fewer times per year. Also, for new investors, "lock-up" periods can be up to two years in which no redemptions can occur.

- *Fees.* Managers receive incentive fees that could reach 20% or more of the profits depending on the fund's return. This payout is in addition to the AUM fees.

1.11. WHAT SHOULD AN INVESTOR CONSIDER WHEN PERFORMING DUE DILIGENCE ON HEDGE FUNDS IN THE FUND SELECTION PROCESS?

Trying to narrow the choices for hedge fund selection can be a daunting task for investors. Thousands of hedge funds exist as possible candidates for investment. As a means of reducing the initial universe of hedge funds for consideration, investors should actively network. You should begin with your professional networks within the investment community as a source of information for a reduced subset adhering to warnings about managers to avoid. This process may help prevent "recreating the wheel" as others may have examined the same hedge fund previously and can offer insights about their findings.

Another common technique you can use during the due diligence process involves engaging hedge fund investors in conversations with those knowledgeable about specific hedge funds. For example, suppose a manager says he works with a particular counterparty or service provider. In that case, you shouldn't only confirm the relationship but also try to have a conversation with the other party. Such a discussion is often informative and provides a different perspective of the hedge fund manager. Many investors garner better information during the due diligence process by interviewing those making up the support network of hedge funds, including prime brokers and lawyers. A *prime broker* provides financing for the hedge fund's long positions and short-selling positions. Such conversations can help affirm claims about procedures and processes undertaken by the hedge fund manager. You should also seek to monitor conference calls, engage in focused reviews, and participate in on-site visits. A balance exists between being overbearing and requesting reasonable transparency. You shouldn't be afraid to ask questions because you may identify an issue the manager has not encountered previously.

Some parts of the due diligence process may be well beyond your expertise as an investor, particularly on operational issues such as legal, compliance, valuation, risk management, and information technology. In these cases, you shouldn't be hesitant to work with experts who have specialized knowledge. In general, you should be concerned about whether appropriate resources exist for staffing levels, whether qualifications have been reviewed and vetted, whether operational risks seem material, and if excessive turnover may jeopardize strategy success.

1.12. HOW IS A HEDGE FUND'S PERFORMANCE MEASURED?

Evaluating a hedge fund's performance requires understanding how hedge funds are classified. For example, some funds try to eliminate market risk while others exploit it. Benchmarking performance requires evaluating performance based on the nature of the strategy. Here are some standard measures used to assess hedge fund performance.

- *Absolute returns.* Comparing absolute returns is appropriate for hedge fund strategies that attempt to eliminate or mitigate market risk focusing on security selection (market-neutral funds). Absolute return benchmarks require establishing an expected range of returns for a strategy and using it for comparison. For a

> *"Although caution is advisable for buyers of hedge fund shares, investors can distinguish talented managers from the merely lucky by using refined performance measurement techniques."*
> David M. Smith

market-neutral strategy, the only component of return left is the mispricing of securities since market risk has been eliminated or substantially reduced. Firms often use leverage to augment returns. A fund manager could establish a successful market neutral strategy based on the ability to earn a return above some specified level.

- *Risk-adjusted performance.* Assessing performance on a level playing field involves making an apples-to-apples comparison, requiring adjusting returns for the risk taken. The most common risk-adjusted performance measure is the *Sharpe ratio*, which is the excess return (the fund's return minus the risk-free rate) divided by the fund's returns' standard deviation. The *risk-free rate* is the return generated by a riskless investment, typically a government-issued Treasury security. Because the Sharpe ratio is a relative measure, you must compare one fund's Sharpe ratio to another, not a particular value. Higher Sharpe ratios indicate better risk-adjusted performance.

• *Hedge fund benchmarks.* Benchmarks offer a relative, rather than an absolute, return comparison. Organizations such as Hedge Fund Research (https://www.hedgefundresearch. com/) provide aggregated indices based on various hedge fund strategy classifications. For example, for event-driven strategies, Hedge Fund Research offers a merger arbitrage index and an activist index, to name a few. Hedge fund benchmarks are often constructed based on self-reporting of funds claiming a given style. Data are aggregated and serve as a potential means of comparison. Finding a fund that consistently performs in the top quartile (upper 25%) is a good goal.

• *Downside capture. Downside capture* is a statistical measure of an investment manager's overall performance in down-markets. Calculating this ratio involves dividing the fund manager's returns by the corresponding index returns during the down-market and multiplying that factor by 100. This ratio is useful in evaluating how well an investment manager performed relative to an index during periods when that index has dropped. If an investment manager has a downside capture ratio of less than 100, this result indicates that the manager outperformed the index during the down-market. For instance, a manager who has a downside capture ratio of 75 shows that the portfolio declined only 75% as much as the index during the specified period. Thus, the lower the downside capture ratio, the more likely a fund can cope with a large market decline. Because many hedge funds pursue strategies that intentionally deviate from exposure to market risks, downside capture may be an inappropriate measure to consider when evaluating risks.

1.13. HOW HAVE HEDGE FUNDS PERFORMED SINCE THE 1990s?

Categorizing hedge fund performance can be misleading due to the range of styles used by hedge fund managers. Some strategies, such as those for equity hedge funds, are tied strongly to the overall pattern of market returns. Others, such as market-neutral funds, have returns independent of overall market performance. Most arbitrage strategies depend on relative mispricing between closely related securities. Nevertheless, some patterns have emerged on hedge fund returns since the 1990s.

From the early 1990s until 2002, hedge funds offered returns comparable with equity securities, but with much less risk. The risk levels were much more in line with those of bonds. Also, most strategies during this period provided liquidity to the market, which the market tends to reward with a performance premium.

Between 2003 and the end of the financial crisis of 2007–2008,, hedge fund returns moderated, performing well on a relative basis, but not as well on an absolute basis. Part of the shift was due to the role hedge funds played during that period as their strategies became more liquidity demanding than liquidity supplying. In other words, during this period, hedge funds pursued strategies that were more in line with market trends. Increasing overall risk negated some of the advantages that existed within many hedge fund strategies.

In the aftermath of the financial crisis, namely, 2009 to the present, hedge fund returns deteriorated with the introduction of exchange-traded fund (ETF) strategies such as short selling, which typically was within the domain of hedge funds. Hedge funds underperformed the S&P 500 index each year starting in 2009, with the difference exceeding 20% in 2013. The quantitative easing strategies of countries such as the United States resulted in higher than average correlations among stocks, further challenging other hedge fund strategies. *Quantitative easing* occurs when a central bank buys government-issued securities in the open market to increase the money supply and stimulate the economy. With increased liquidity resulting from government-based stimulus programs, hedge fund strategies have seen their historical role as liquidity suppliers usurped.

1.14. WHAT ARE HEDGE FUND REPLICATION STRATEGIES?

Hedge fund replication strategies try to capture traditional and alternative systematic risk (beta risk) along with returns associated with identifying mispriced securities (alpha risk). Although the traditional systematic risk is associated with the overall market, *alternative systematic risk*, also known as *alternative beta exposure,* introduces sources of return usually unavailable from traditional assets. Overall, the three most common strategies include traditional systematic risk strategies, alternative beta strategies, and bottom-up replication.

- *Traditional systematic risk strategies.* These strategies include risks such as movements in interest rates or stock prices.

- *Alternative beta strategies*. These strategies try to capture extra returns by taking on risks such as credit risk and volatility risk. *Credit risk* is the probability of defaulting on an obligation. *Volatility risk* is the risk of loss associated with a large amount of uncertainty resulting in fluctuations in a security's value. Some strategies use statistical techniques to replicate the return or risk patterns of hedge fund strategies.

- *Bottom-up replication*. These strategies, often enacted by ETFs, attempt to mimic strategy trades that can mirror a hedge fund's returns in the aggregate.

Replication strategies try to mimic hedge fund returns without actually taking on hedge fund exposure. Unlike hedge funds, these replication strategies offer no lock-up periods, greater transparency by disclosing positions, more flexibility by adjusting risk based on preferences, better diversification, more opportunities to take short positions, and lower fees.

One major advantage of replication products is that if properly executed, they can generate an enhanced return. Such returns occur by introducing alternative beta exposure, which, in turn, can improve risk-adjusted return. Likewise, replication products can also diversify risk by capturing returns from strategies with a low correlation with traditional assets. The performance of replication strategies has had mixed reviews. If you can identify a persistent top-tier manager, this manager is worth considering; otherwise, the results often fall short of comparable hedge fund strategies.

> *"If synthetic replication of hedge fund indices is possible, then investors may cheaply obtain broad hedge fund exposure."*
> Mikhail Tupitsyn and Paul Lajbcygier

1.15. WHAT ARE '40 ACT FUNDS, AND HOW CAN INVESTORS USE THEM TO GAIN EXPOSURES SIMILAR TO HEDGE FUNDS?

A *'40 Act Fund* is a PIV issued by a registered investment company as defined by the 1940 Investment Company Act. Congress passed the Investment Company Act of 1940 to regulate investment companies and their permitted activities. The legislation establishes the requirements for publicly traded investment products, including open-end mutual funds, closed-end mutual funds, and unit investment trusts. Hedge funds offered through the US '40 Act mutual fund structure place restrictions on riskier strategies and require increased compliance costs associated with ensuring they're suitable for *retail investors*, who are non-professional individual investors.

By converting to a mutual fund, hedge fund managers can use their hedge fund's performance record to attract new investors. Raising capital for hedge funds is challenging as their clientele is limited to high net-worth individuals and institutional investors willing to pay an AUM fee and an incentive fee. Many investors want to limit the amount of illiquid investments they hold. Most hedge funds provide monthly valuations, which restrict their distribution to these high net-worth investors.

Thus, registered '40 Act Funds offer a larger distribution base with fewer entry barriers for the average shareholder. By converting to a mutual fund, the hedge fund manager can attract new investors. A mutual fund can offer a low minimum investment, improved liquidity, and increased transparency into the fund's assets. Examples of '40 Act funds with alternative strategies include Securian AM Dynamic Managed Vol Fd (VVMIX), Dunham Dynamic Macro Fund (DNAVX), and OnTrack Core Fund (OTRFX).

1.16. HOW DO FUNDS OF HEDGE FUNDS DIFFER FROM MULTI-STRATEGY FUNDS?

Gaining access to the best performing managers is challenging for individual investors, but FOF managers can provide this access as a part of their hedge funds portfolio. By investing across a pool of hedge funds, a FOF reduces the risks of having all your money tied up with an individual manager. Besides providing diversification to reduce overall risk, a FOF also offers liquidity to allow for new investments and enables redemptions more readily upon request. However, diversification comes at a price: an additional layer of fees. The individual hedge funds in which the FOF manager invests and the FOF manager receive both management and incentive fees. Typically, a FOF underperforms reported hedge fund indices. These results may be misleading because some consider index performance to be inaccurate. After all, funds self-report, and underperforming hedge funds aren't likely to report. In general, the performance of a FOF tends to be more reflective of actual hedge fund performance. Examples of FOF include BAAM, UBS Hedge Fund Solutions1, and Goldman Sachs Asset Management.

Multi-strategy funds are funds within the same organization that invest across various hedge fund strategies, thus providing diversification within a hedge fund. By doing so, they avoid the second level of fees associated with a FOF. They also engage in fee netting, meaning they aggregate overall performance to assess the

> "Multistrategy hedge funds have a special status in the world of hedge funds because they offer a diversified hedge fund exposure to investors."
> Paul-Henri Bayart De-Germont and Daniel Capocci

incentive fees. Multi-strategy funds are often capable of quickly shifting strategies if needed because they're all within the same corporate structure and can offer superior risk management. HBK Capital Management, Tudor Investment Corporation, and Wellington Management Company LLP are examples of multi-strategy funds.

1.17. WHY IS MANAGER SELECTION A CRITICAL CONSIDERATION IN PICKING HEDGE FUNDS?

Manager selection is an essential consideration in selecting hedge funds. Some research indicates that managers exhibit *return persistence*, meaning those with excellent performance are more likely to be among the next period's best performers. Investors often classify performance for hedge fund managers by quartile. A *quartile* consists of four equal groups by dividing a population according to the returns generated. Thus, a top quartile manager would indicate that a manager's performance is among the top 25% of all funds within a particular peer group. A *peer group* reflects funds that follow a similar investing strategy such as global macro or merger arbitrage. Top quartile managers have a greater likelihood of repeating as top-quartile managers for the next year and may continue to do so for an extended period. This performance persistence is related to fund strategies and characteristics such as fund size, the similarity in cash flow patterns, fees, flow restrictions, and across strategies. As an investor in a hedge fund, hedge fund replication strategy, or a FOF strategy, performance persistence has important implications for investment decisions. In particular, you should consider a manager's track record in selecting hedge funds.

1.18. WHAT TRAITS ARE GENERALLY ASSOCIATED WITH SUCCESSFUL HEDGE FUND MANAGERS?

You can differentiate successful hedge fund managers based on their education, professional experience, social capital, risk management skills, and self-improvement skills.

- *Education and professional experience.* Fund managers obtain educational skills through formal and informal outlets. Academic aptitude and advanced degrees are associated with better fund performance. Informal education includes the ability to adapt to changing market dynamics, technology, and strategies. Industry experience is often associated with better results. For hedge fund managers, it's a mixed bag. To gain a reputation in this industry, new entrants may devote more time and effort than experienced managers. Once establishing a reputation, fund managers often need to exert less effort to maintain that reputation. Also, managers with more experience frequently exhibit higher risk aversion, which results in less volatility, but lower returns.

- *Social capital.* *Social capital* represents the networks of relationships among people who live and work in a particular society or social setting, which improves the effectiveness of some activity or desired outcome. For the hedge fund industry, the best representation of social capital is the breadth and strength of these professional connections. This social capital assists in the flow of information, which can add more value. Thus, managers with higher social capital have an advantage over counterparts who lack professional networks. Social capital consists of structural capital, relational capital, and cognitive capital.

o *Structural capital* refers to the interconnectedness of hedge fund team members. It reflects how effectively each team member communicates the information and coordinates task execution. Structural capital should enable the communication of information in the most efficient manner. A successful hedge fund should be led by managers who share a team orientation in which skill sets are complementary across the team. Team members should also focus on task execution, which requires trust.

o *Relational capital* refers to successful interactions with others to achieve common personal goals. A successful hedge fund manager enhances the development of these relationships, which can lead to increased value added in fund performance.

o *Cognitive capital* refers to shared social norms, values, and language. Shared values can lead to more positive attitudes, which may better facilitate communication and thus enhance information exchange as it reduces possible misunderstanding. More efficient information exchange can lead to a hedge fund manager's ability to generate alpha. *Alpha* is a measure of performance, representing the excess return of an investment relative to an appropriate benchmark return.

- *Risk management skills.* Risk management skills allow for effective comparisons of risks and uncertainties. If managers can identify and act on over-discounted risks while identifying and avoiding risks not yet anticipated by the market, they should have superior performance. Hedge fund managers generally operate in a dynamic environment where the trade-offs between risk and return change rapidly.

- *Self-development skills.* Self-development skills are among the essential traits that a manager should possess.

Hedge fund managers must exhibit restraint to avoid being overtaken by emotions through challenging market conditions; otherwise, they may miss alpha-generating opportunities. *Alpha generating strategies* are strategies that create excess returns or returns that exceed a benchmark. A hedge fund manager detached from the emotions that arise during the investment process can judge more objectively and see the issues from a clearer perspective.

1.19. WHAT ROLES DO HEDGE FUNDS PLAY IN THE ACTIVIST INVESTING MOVEMENT?

An *activist investor* is an individual or group that acquires a substantial percentage of a public company's shares to effect change within the company. Historically, activist institutional investors such as pension funds were the primary protagonists for change. More recently, hedge funds have joined the activist movement. Activist hedge funds choose to target mismanaged firms to control the target firm's board to address its problems. If successful, these hedge funds establish a goal to make the target firms more profitable, generating higher returns for their funds.

Strategies employed by activist shareholders include corrective mechanisms such as seeking out better investments, spinning off strategic divestitures, evaluating shareholder value-maximizing payout policies, altering the capital structure, and improving corporate governance. If the target company's management is unwilling to cooperate, activist hedge funds may engage in a proxy fight, resulting in higher costs. A *proxy fight* is a competitive struggle between two factions, such as activist and management, for the shareholders' proxy votes needed to control a corporation. During a proxy fight, the activist hedge fund often enjoys greater credibility with the other shareholders than the existing management because activists' goals align with those of the shareholders.

Hedge fund activists' goal is to intervene in the target firm's specific corporate policies to enhance managerial efficiency but not acquire it. As such, hedge fund activists' goal is to boost firm value by reducing managerial entrenchment and resolving managerial agency problems, improving operational efficiency, and increasing expected takeover premiums.

1.20. WHAT ARE THE PRIMARY CONCERNS INVESTORS SHOULD CONSIDER BEFORE INVESTING IN HEDGE FUNDS?

Hedge fund investing is often controversial. The lack of transparency and the reduced accessibility of hedge funds to ordinary investors contribute to their mystique. Obtaining information on hedge fund returns may be challenging since hedge funds aren't required to report returns and may choose not to do so when returns are bad. Since overall hedge fund returns have declined since the financial crisis of 2007–2008, investors increasingly believe that they aren't worth the high fees charged. Furthermore, hedge funds remain largely unregulated. Some blame hedge funds for causing a severe systemic risk to global financial markets based on extensively using leverage and relatively higher levels of failures. *Systemic risk* is the risk that one financial institution's failure could cause related institutions to fail, leading to widespread harm to the overall economy.

You should carefully consider if your portfolio objectives align with allocating products that offer hedge fund exposure. Investor education is also essential to understand some of the more complex strategies that hedge funds often employ.

1.21. SHOULD YOU INVEST IN HEDGE FUNDS?

For most individual investors, the question of investing directly in hedge funds is likely a moot point. Why? Anyone investing with a hedge fund must qualify as an accredited investor. Even if you are eligible, you should avoid hedge funds unless you have thoroughly conducted your due diligence and understand the substantial risks and drawbacks of such investments. You probably should leave investing in hedge funds to institutional and highly knowledgeable high net-worth investors. If you decide to invest in hedge funds, they should represent a small portion of your portfolio.

1.22. WHAT ARE SOME ONLINE RESOURCES FOR HEDGE FUNDS?

Several online resources are available if you're considering hedge fund exposure.

- The *SEC* (https://www.investor.gov/introduction-investing/basics/investment-products/hedge-funds) offers an explanation of hedge funds and items for consideration before investing.

- *Morningstar* (http://corporate.morningstar.com/US/asp/subject.aspx?xmlfile=545.xml) provides relevant data on more than 7,000 hedge funds.

- *Barclays* (https://www.barclayhedge.com/category/resources/definitions/) explains the terminology associated with hedge fund investing.

TAKEAWAYS

Hedge funds offer an opportunity for savvy investors to gain access to strategies and exposures unavailable through traditional investment options to potentially increase portfolio returns. If you meet the guidelines for accredited investors and are ready to invest in a hedge fund, consider the following tips:

- Understand how hedge funds fit into your total portfolio.

- Review the hedge fund with a financial advisor's help to ensure that it is suitable for your investment objectives and investment period.

- Read through fund prospectuses carefully before making such investments as hedge funds vary substantially regarding risk and return.

- Make sure the strategy or strategies used by the hedge fund meet your long-term needs.

- Make sure that the fund's share redemption timetable meets your personal financial needs.

- Understand your fee obligations, including both management and incentive fees.

- Be aware that funds of hedge funds can be costly as you're paying two sets of fees but offer risk reduction through diversification.

- Look for a track record of sustained success and a reliable management team.

- Compare the hedge fund's returns with others following a similar strategy or strategies.

- Research the fund manager before you invest any money by checking out the advisor/manager's Form ADV, which is available on the SEC's IAPD website.

- Consider obtaining indirect access through hedge fund replication products that mimic hedge fund strategies.

2

PRIVATE EQUITY: INVESTING FOR LONGER-TERM OPPORTUNITIES

> *"It's important that we educate Americans about how hedge funds and private equity play completely different roles."*
> Stephen A. Schwarzman, American Businessman

The elements behind private equity (PE) – external financing, high risk, but a high return potential based on competitive advantage – go back well into the previous millennium. The pitch that Christopher Columbus made to Ferdinand II of Aragon and Isabella I of Castile to sponsor his trip to the West meets these criteria. More formally, PE made its debut at the beginning of the industrial revolution. In 1854, London and Paris merchant bankers Jacob and Isaac Pereire,

> *"In the 1930s, there was a stretch where you could borrow more against the real estate than you could sell it for. I think that's what's going in in today's private-equity world."*
> Charlie Munger

along with Jay Cooke from New York, founded Crédit Mobilier to provide financing for the United States Transcontinental Railroad.

PE encompasses a broad set of investments consisting of venture capital (VC) and buyout or leveraged buyout (LBO) funds. *VC* is the structure used to finance start-up companies or expand businesses that generally have limited access to other funding sources. A *buyout fund* uses money from investors to buy other companies, sometimes taking publicly-traded companies private to avoid the scrutiny of public markets. In 1901, the first buyout transaction occurred as Andrew Carnegie sold his steel company to J. P. Morgan. Wealthy individuals and families dominated the PE market for the first half of the 1900s. In 1946, the first modern PE fund began with the formation of the American Research and Development Corporation and J. H. Whitney & Company. The Small Business Investment Act of 1958 opened the gateway for VC firms to structure as Small Business Investment Companies (SBICs) or Minority Enterprise SBICs, which became eligible for federal funds. In the two decades that followed, most VC firms focused on technology.

Meanwhile, buyout funds also expanded. In 1955, the first LBO occurred with McLean Industries, Inc, which began a trend during the 1960s of acquiring publicly-traded holding companies. A *LBO* happens when one company buys another company using a substantial amount – typically about 90% – of borrowed money.

By 1989, the PE industry had raised $21.9 billion. PE continued to grow until immediately before the financial crisis of 2007–2008 and then slowed in the aftermath. According to data from industry tracker Preqin, the global PE industry raised more than half a trillion dollars in 2019. These new funds, along with an 11% increase in unrealized value, increased assets under management (AUM) to $4.11

trillion as of June 2019. As of June 30, 2019, Cambridge Associates reported a 25-year annualized PE Index return of 13.52% compared to the S & P 500 index of 9.97%.

"Private-equity and hedge-fund guys typically come into a situation of mediocrity, where rapid change may result in a profit."
Austin Ligon

Having covered the history of PE, let's now enter the fascinating but often misunderstood world of these pooled investment vehicles (PIVs). Like hedge funds, only accredited investors, who have enough knowledge and experience to engage in such investments, can invest in PE. Chapter 1 described the requirements for accredited investor status.

2.1. WHAT IS PE, AND HOW DOES IT WORK?

PE refers to a closed-end investment fund organized as a limited partnership that doesn't trade on a public exchange. Institutional investors and private wealth clients serve as investors (limited partners or LPs), and the PE firm serves as the manager (general partner or GP). Usually, only one GP has control over the management of the limited partnership. The GP also has unlimited liability to third parties for the debts and obligations of the limited partnership. PE funds invest in private start-up companies called VC or engage in public companies' buyouts (buyout funds). PE investments are typically sold or liquidated within 10 years.

"Private equity helps produce strong companies, promotes innovation and spurs job growth."
N. Robert Hammer

Their returns usually result from an initial public offering (IPO), a merger or sale, or a recapitalization. A *recapitalization* represents the process of restructuring a company's mix of debt and equity to create more financial stability. In the past, transferring PE ownership was challenging because an investor would have to find a buyer since a formal marketplace didn't exist.

2.2. HOW DOES PE DIFFER FROM A HEDGE FUND?

Historically, hedge funds often have objectives associated with quickly generating the highest possible return investing in liquid assets. Their focus is to maximize short-term profits and then shift to other investments that also offer the possibility of a quick return. In contrast, PE funds focus on improving longer-term opportunities through enhancing management skills, streamlining operations, and engaging in expansions. Their goal is to sell companies at a profit. Since the early 2000s, distinctions still exist, but the lines have blurred somewhat.

2.3. HOW DOES PE DIFFER FROM PUBLIC EQUITY?

Both PE and public equity represent ownership in a company that appears on a company's balance sheet under shareholder's equity. Companies use equity to acquire assets, pay off debt, and execute transactions that enable them to grow. The structure of PE and public equity offerings differ based on return structure and voting privileges. Public equity is initially issued by the company, often with the assistance of investment banking firms. Once issued, investors can trade public equity in a *secondary market,* where investors buy and sell securities previously issued. Stocks of publicly-traded firms tend to be followed by financial analysts who provide considerable information to the capital markets in addition to the financial information required by regulatory authorities. Public stocks tend to be highly *liquid*, meaning that stockholders can easily find someone else to buy some or all of their ownership stake. Owners of public equity can choose to hold their stock for a short time to indefinitely.

> *"People used to think that private equity was basically just a compensation scheme, but it much more about making companies more efficient."*
> David Rubenstein

PE investing is available only to *accredited investors*, who are sophisticated investors meeting minimum income or net worth requirements as detailed in Chapter 1. Little information is available to PE investors outside that supplied by the GP. Once becoming an LP, transferring such ownership can often require owners to take a deep discount if they can't locate another buyer. Unless PE owners can transfer ownership, they face an extended period of ownership. However, the ownership is finite and limited to the PE fund's life span, typically 7 to 10 years. Little regulatory oversight protects PE owners.

> *"Private equity has been the purview of super wealthy individuals and institutions."*
> Michael Lee-Chin

2.4. WHY IS PE IMPORTANT TO THE FINANCIAL INDUSTRY AND SOCIETY IN GENERAL?

PE serves a valuable function in society by providing ownership capital to promising organizations that otherwise would not have access. In their infancy, most companies rely on funding from their founders and others closely associated with the founders, known *as angel investors*. These companies may only be working on prototypes with no actual product for sale. Access to public equity is impossible at this stage, because these organizations lack sufficient development. PE through VC offers the opportunity to take these companies to the next level – to obtain additional equity funding to continue their journey toward becoming more mature businesses. The earlier PE investors enter into the process, the greater are their risks and potential returns. If these companies successfully advance through the PE process, they may eventually become publicly traded. According to Shikhar Ghosh, a senior lecturer at Harvard Business School, about 75% of PE start-ups never generate a positive return for investors. Almost half liquidate their assets out of this group, causing VC investors to lose their original investments. What motivates these PE investors to take such high risks? Successful companies often produce astronomical returns, which hopefully offset the losses from the unsuccessful ones. For example, Yale University's Endowment Fund invested $300,000 in Google that has returned over $1 billion.

On the other end of the spectrum, public companies can often become mismanaged with a bloated infrastructure or lack of strategic focus. Such features make them, at best uncompetitive and, at worst, candidates for eventual failure. PE through a friendly buyout allows publicly-traded firms to obtain the necessary funds to acquire the shares of existing shareholders, take the firm out of the public purview, and focus on making the required improvements to become a more efficient organization. These changes may include making major changes to the firm's management or selling off unprofitable divisions. About a third of these organizations eventually return to the public markets, such as Dell, with the rest remaining in private hands.

2.5. WHAT ADVANTAGES DOES PE OFFER INVESTORS?

You may want to consider PE for several reasons.

- *Unique exposure.* More than 99% of companies in the United States are in private hands. By only focusing on public firms, you miss out on a vast pool of investment opportunities. Keep in mind that analysts don't review these private firms as extensively as public firms. As such, the chances of identifying an undervalued private investment opportunity are much greater than from a public one. An active secondary market allows market forces to determine an asset's appropriate value. In contrast, the lack of an active PE secondary market means more opportunities to identify undervalued assets.

- *Active role.* PE firms take an active role in managing the companies within their portfolios. They serve as advisors to the firms and make recommendations on firm management. PE firms often invest their own money in the fund. As such, investors align their financial interests with the success of the firms within the fund. Keep in mind that investors in public companies have much less influence on company management other than the ability to vote.

- *Strategic timing.* Unlike mutual funds that must invest based on the net inflows coming into the fund, PE firms aren't under the same pressure. Their ability to delay investments until a more favorable time is a process known as *dry powder* or money that sits in the queue waiting for the fund to invest.

2.6. WHAT DISADVANTAGES OR DRAWBACKS DOES PE OFFER INVESTORS?

Although PE exposure can be enticing, you want to be cautious about this investment for several reasons.

- *Illiquidity*. You are locking up your capital for 7–10 years, which means a limited ability to sell your position. Historically, the ability to cash out of your investment required the approval of other investors. Often exiting investors receive far less than what their investment is worth when cashing out early. Although a secondary market has recently developed offering more choices for entering and exiting positions, it's in its early stage, so these options are still limited.

- *Large investment required*. Direct PE access is limited mainly to institutional investors and high-net-worth individuals. Gaining access requires a substantial initial investment. More recently, indirect access is becoming more commonplace through PE funds.

- *High costs*. Investors – the LPs – must pay both management and incentive fees to the GP. This fee structure is expensive. Historically, investors referred to the structure as 2/20 (2% of AUM and 20% of profits), although the trend is toward fee compression.

- *High risk*. Most investments undertaken by PE managers, especially with VC firms, are high-risk investments. In other words, with VC firms, only a minority of investments becomes profitable. Ideally, these profitable investments more than offset many losers. Additionally, the rate of return between the best and worst-performing firms is wide, which is another indication of risk.

- *Valuation*. Valuation is difficult because PE lacks a public market that puts a value on the firms. Also, the return changes over time as the fate of investments become better known.

2.7. HOW DOES VC WORK?

VC is a type of PE financing provided to start-ups or small businesses perceived to have strong long-term growth potential. Often, these companies can't get funds from banks or borrow from other sources. However, VC investors are willing to take on the higher risk to potentially achieve above-average returns. Table 2.1 shows that

> *"Private equity finds a substantial amount of new businesses and is the source of capital to rejuvenate failing businesses, which are major drivers of job growth in this economy."*
> N. Robert Hammer

a VC's life consists of stages along the VC continuum. A limited partnership agreement (LPA) usually serves as the basis for structuring buyout firms. This agreement outlines the role of investors (LPs) and management (GP). The life expectancy of these partnerships ranges from 7 to 10 years, with the ability to extend several additional years. The VC fund's goal is to take a company public through an IPO or to cash out in some other fashion, such as through a merger or acquisition. The LPs contribute capital to the fund, but they may face additional capital calls when the GP is ready to invest. A *capital call* requires the LPs to honor their financial commitments at the time of the call. These calls usually occur during the first 3–5 years. Besides selecting investments, the GP also provides operational expertise to assist the business owners while gaining market share in the new or high growth industry.

> *"Venture capital is about capturing the value between the startup phase and the public company phase."*
> Fred Wilson

Table 2.1. Five Stages of Venture Capital

Stage	Description
Seed capital	At this stage, the start-up typically doesn't have a commercially available product. The start-up's efforts lean toward convincing potential funders that its ideas are worth supporting. Funding comes in rounds, with recipients having to show some progress before receiving additional funding. At this stage, the start-up often uses the money to conduct market research or to add more personnel
Start-up capital	Following market analysis and completing a business plan, this funding stage often focuses on marketing by advertising products and acquiring customers. Products are typically developed at this stage, although the start-up can use the funding for necessary improvements
Manufacturing and sales	The third stage features more substantial funding, because investments are needed to obtain production facilities and to generate sales through effective marketing campaigns. This stage is the first opportunity for some companies to start generating a profit
Expansion	The start-up often dedicates funding at this stage to product differentiation and market expansion. Product differentiation also launches diversification strategies. Companies at this point have been operating for at least several years
Pre-IPO	In the final stage, companies are preparing for a possible IPO or potential acquisition. They can also use funds to effectively drive out competitors or establish a more competitive price structure

Examples of VC funds include Sequoia Capital, Accel Partners, Benchmark Capital, Greylock Partners, and LOWERCASE Capital.

Traditional valuation methods don't work with VC due to the lack of a public market for valuation. Investors and analysts assess returns through a measure known as the *interim* (or since inception) *internal rate of return* (IRR), which reflects returns earned to date and incorporates an estimate of future earnings through assessing *net asset value* (NAV), which is the difference between a firm's assets and liabilities.

2.8. WHAT FEATURES DOES AN LPA TYPICALLY COVER?

An LPA aligns the partners' interests. This agreement typically contains two types of clauses. *Economic clauses* cover GP contributions known as "hurt money" and management fees, expenses, and the distribution *waterfall*, which indicates the payment of incentive fees. *Investor protection clauses* cover fund strategy, termination requirements, investment committee, and LP advisory committee. Descriptions of the more common clauses follow:

- *Hurdle rate*. The *hurdle rate*, also known as the *preferred* (or "pref") *return*, is the return that the fund must earn before the GP can receive incentive fees. The hurdle rate incentivizes the manager to outperform and potentially aligns the GP and LPs' interests. However, a concern exists for excessive risk-taking on the GP's part to increase the likelihood of earning incentive fees.

- *Hurt money*. *Hurt money* represents a requirement in the LPA for the GP to also invest in the fund. This provision's logic is that if the GP is an investor, then the GP's wealth is also tied to the fund's success. Consequently, hurt money incentivizes the GP to work hard to earn maximum returns for the fund without taking an excessive risk that would endanger the GP's wealth.

- *Distribution waterfall*. The distribution waterfall outlines the distribution of incentive fees between the participants in an investment. As noted previously, the hurdle rate establishes the fund's return before the GP can receive incentive fees. The distribution waterfall outlines the allocation of returns between the LPs, who receive invested capital plus the total return up to the hurdle rate and the GP who receives incentive fees once achieving the hurdle rate. Once the GP meets the hurdle rate, the payment of incentive fees starts based on the catch-up provision. A *catch-up provision* establishes how quickly the GP received returns above the incentive rate. For example, with a 100% catch-up, the GP receives 100% of all profits above the hurdle rate until the GP's total incentive fees approach the incentive fee rate (e.g., 20%). For example, while the LPs receive the first 10% (as a hurdle rate) if the GP operates under a 100% catch-up rate on a 20% incentive fee, the GP would receive the next 2.5% to "catch-up" to the LP return. At this point, the GP earns 20% of the total profits (2.5%/12.5% = 0.20 or 20%). For any profits above 12.5%, the fund would distribute 80% to the LPs and 20% to the GP.

- *Clawback clause.* A *clawback clause* requires the GP to return early incentive fees to the LPs if subsequent performance is poor. Clawback provisions are relatively rare in LPAs due to the possible litigation costs required to ensure that the GP returns the incentive fees.

- *Distribution provision.* A *distribution provision* establishes the timing for the sharing of the profits. The two most common methods are the *deal-by-deal basis* and the *fund-as-a-whole basis*. The deal-by-deal basis rewards the GP based on each project at its conclusion. If a project generates a return that exceeds the hurdle rate, the GP receives an incentive fee. If a project doesn't exceed the hurdle rate, then the GP earns no incentive fee.

The fund-as-a-whole basis rewards the GP based on the aggregated performance of all deals. Thus, unprofitable projects don't detract from the incentive fees paid for profitable projects under deal-by-deal. This arrangement could encourage GPs to liquidate profitable projects early to collect incentive fees. However, under the fund-as-a-whole, unprofitable projects can offset gains for profitable ones when calculating incentive fees.

- *Termination clauses.* A *termination clause* establishes procedures for replacing the GP for underperformance based on a bad-leaver clause (for cause removal) or a good-leaver clause (without cause). Good-leaver clauses require a higher percentage of support of LPs than do bad-leaver clauses to execute.

2.9. WHAT ARE CO-INVESTMENTS, AND HOW CAN THEY POTENTIALLY HELP OR HURT INVESTORS?

Co-investment occurs when the LP invests directly in a portfolio company alongside the GP representing the fund. With co-investment, the GP invites the LP to directly invest in the target company, beyond the LP's exposure through the fund. Since the co-investment occurs outside the fund, the co-investment opportunity isn't subject to the GP fee structure. The co-investment reduces company exposure for the GP, who secures the outside investment opportunities for the LPs. The primary concern with this arrangement is that the GP invites the LP to invest in lower-quality deals. The advantages for investors associated with co-investing include:

- lower fees on a percentage basis due to co-investment being outside the fund's fee structure;

- outsourced screening for the co-investment opportunity to the GP; and

- reduction in the J-curve effect since the co-investment portion doesn't require the payment of fees to the GP, which drives negative performance in the years before harvesting (selling off investments) occurs.

The *J-curve effect* is a graphic relation of time versus return describing the typical trajectory of returns generated by a PE firm. PE portfolios require substantial funding upfront to retool a company, initially resulting in negative returns. However, by harvesting the rewards of the PE firm's efforts for successful firms, a steep improvement occurs in PE performance resulting in an increasing IRR. Figure 2.1 illustrates the J-curve effect.

The disadvantages of co-investing include:

- *Conflicts of interest.* The GP has a vested interest in creating additional demand for the company in question.

- *Reduced diversification.* Unbalanced portfolios for the LP could occur from investing outside the fund resulting in reduced diversification.

- *Increased fiduciary risk.* Increased risk occurs as a more concentrated portion of the LP wealth is tied up with the GP. *Fiduciary risk* is the risk that the GP fails to act in the LP's best interest.

> *"Buyout funds have established themselves as an important factor on the market for corporate control, as well as an important asset class to institutional investors and high net-worth individuals."*
>
> Christian Rauch and
> Marc P. Umber

2.10. WHAT IS A BUYOUT FUND?

A *buyout fund* purchases publicly-traded companies and sometimes takes them private. Its goal is to make a company more profitable and then sell it or take it public for a profit. Ideally, by taking a company out of the public eye, buyout funds can renew its entrepreneurial spirit by pursuing new business lines or drastic cost-cutting measures. Simultaneously, a buyout fund can address issues related to unprofitable divisions, potentially reducing staff and cutting costs, and thus streamlining business operations. As a buyout fund looks to restructure its target firms, it also seeks to improve corporate governance. Improved governance includes clarifying the board's role, monitoring organizational performance, establishing a risk management framework, and enhancing skills for and communicating relevant information to the board. Most buyout funds take on considerable debt when privatizing, which increases their riskiness, especially if they can't effectively reduce their costs. Hence, they are called LBOs.

Unlike VC firms, buyout firms (funds) focus on more developed product markets with well-known product demand. Consequently, buyout firms are usually much larger than VC firms, reflecting their target investments' relative size. Acquired buyout companies have professional managers and established revenue streams. Their returns are more predictable than those of VC firms, and buyout firms often use leverage to augment returns.

Buyout funds are structured in the same manner as VC funds through an LPA with an average life span of about six years. At this point, the buyout fund (1) sells to another buyout firm, (2) identifies a strategic buyer, (3) becomes a public firm again through an IPO, or (4) takes on more debt by the current owners through another LBO. Examples of buyout funds include Sun Capital Partners, Thoma Bravo Fund, Vista

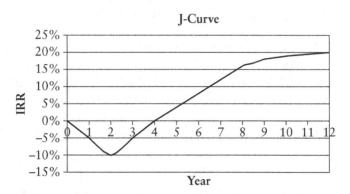

Figure 2.1.   J-Curve Effect
Source: Available at http://www.allenlatta.com/uploads/9/1/8/6/9186389/
editor/j-curve-1.jpg?1499547630

Equity Partners Fund, Harvest Partners, and KPS Special Situations Fund.

2.11. WHAT MAIN RISKS DO PE FIRMS FACE?

PE firms encounter four main risks.

• *Market risk*. *Market risk* is the economic uncertainty regarding valuation. Although most PE funds don't trade actively in the secondary market, valuations are often related to what's happening in public markets. Since PE investments are more return enhancers than diversifiers, a high correlation exists with the broad equity market.

• *Liquidity risk*. Because investments extend for the duration of the limited partnership, LPs face substantial liquidity risk. Traditionally, PE firms penalized LPs who had the approval to sell their partnership interest with a hefty discount when exiting because of the investments' illiquid nature. With a developing secondary market, the size of these discounts should decrease over time.

- *Funding risk*. *Funding risk* is the risk associated with the unpredictable timing of cash flows over the fund's life. Projections of entry or exit points with individual products are estimates.

- *Capital risk*. *Capital risk* is the risk that a fund may be unable to recover its invested capital.

2.12. WHAT DO THE TERMS DRAWDOWN AND VINTAGE YEAR MEAN?

Drawdown, also known as a *capital call*, occurs when the GP notifies the LPs of a need for funds for new investment and requires the LPs to honor their commitments to contribute to the investment. *Vintage year* refers to the first year that a drawdown occurs. When comparing PE funds' performance, you should compare against other funds from the same vintage year because overall fund returns heavily depend on the investment's time frame. In other words, investing when opportunities are cheap can mean higher returns, while investing when opportunities are expensive can result in lower returns.

2.13. HOW CAN INVESTORS WITH LIMITED CAPITAL ACCESS THE PE MARKET?

If you have a defined benefit plan with your employer, it's likely you already have exposure to PE. A *defined benefit plan*

> *"In the '70s and '80s, what private equity did is it changed corporate America. It started holding companies accountable, and for the first time managers started thinking like owners."*
>
> Henry Kravis

provides a fixed, pre-established benefit for employees at retirement. Why? Pension funds, university endowments, and foundations hold about 70% of the investments made in the largest 100 PE firms. Given that you must be an accredited investor to invest individually, you can also obtain exposure to PE through exchange-traded funds (ETFs) but with much lower investment levels. Examples of PE ETFs include Invesco Global Listed Private Equity Portfolio (NYSE Arca: PSP) and ProShares Global Listed Private Equity (CBOE BZX: PEX).

2.14. HOW IS THE PERFORMANCE FOR PE INVESTMENTS BENCHMARKED?

Conventional methods of measuring performance don't readily apply to PE because an active secondary market is still in an early development stage. Thus, the following are common ways to benchmark performance PE investments.

- *Peer groups.* Peer groups or cohorts are the basis of one group of PE measures. With peer groups, you compare return measures against other managers from the same vintage year, and assessment occurs based on the quartile in which the manager's performance falls.

- *Interim IRR.* As mentioned previously, a standard measure for returns is the interim IRR, also known as the since-inception IRR. The *interim IRR* is an estimate of the IRR performance before fund liquidation, with the remaining value estimated based on the NAV.

- *Total value to paid-in (TVPI) ratio.* The *TVPI ratio* looks at the sum of all previous distributions plus an estimate of the NAV divided by the sum of all invested capital. A TVPI greater than one indicates a fund's profitability.

Peer group comparisons are popular but may not reflect actual PE performance because of: (1) self-selection bias because reporting is voluntary among managers, (2) low data quality because of a lack of investible assets, (3) potential double-counting, and (4) valuation bias. Other than peer group comparisons, another type of performance measure identifies public securities as a starting point for comparison. A kind of asset-based measure is using listed PE as a means of comparison. Although this segment is growing, it represents only a small portion of the PE market. Another measure is to take a public equity market index such as the S&P 500 index and add a premium based on a historical or a projected relative difference between the private and public market returns. A third method is what is known as the *public market equivalent (PME) method,* which involves adjusting the return to what an investor would have by investing PE capital calls in a public index.

Using different measures and judgment is essential, given that all measures have potential flaws. For instance, risk differences can exist when comparing PE funds. Constraining manager comparisons to those with assets of the peer group presents challenges, because PE firms aren't transparent and often don't reveal their investments.

2.15. WHAT IS THE REGULATORY FRAMEWORK FOR PE?

The history of PE regulation parallels the previously discussed regulatory framework of hedge funds. The Investment

Advisers Act of 1940 exempted the GP in PE funds if the fund had 15 or fewer clients. With the passage of the Dodd-Frank Act of 2010, all PE firms with more than $150 million in assets must now register with the Securities and Exchange Commission (SEC). PE funds must also report their size, services offered, investors, employees, and any conflicts of interest.

2.16. HOW ARE PE FUNDS TAXED?

Most PE funds are structured as either limited partnerships or limited liability companies (LLCs). Laws require taxing both structures as a partnership, making them *pass-through vehicles*, meaning no taxation occurs at the fund level. Instead, income is "passed through" to investors who report returns on their tax returns. The tax rate for long-term capital gains generated by PE funds is the long-term capital gains rate. In the United States, the tax rate for incentives fees, also known as *carried interest*, for investments held for less than three years is the ordinary income tax rate, not the long-term capital gains rate.

2.17. HOW PREVALENT ARE PE FUNDS AMONG INVESTORS?

According to Preqin, as of January 2020, over 8,400 institutions worldwide invest in PE, representing a 36.14% increase since 2015 when Preqin listed 6,170 institutions as investors. Almost half of these investors are in North America with 4,148, followed by Europe (2,067) and Asia (1,507). In North America, 3,881 of the 4,148 investors (93.56%) resided in the United States (https://www.preqin.com/=).

Likewise, the number of fund managers offering a PE product had increased to more than 18,000 in early 2020, representing a 9.76% increase since 2018 when 16,400 were offering PE products. A total of 3,526 funds were available in January 2020. The biggest funds are getting bigger – the 20 largest funds captured 45% of all the committed capital in 2019, up from 29% in 2014. As of March 2020, the five largest PE funds were The Blackstone Group Inc, Neuberger Berman Group LLC, Apollo Global Management Inc, Carlyle Group Inc, and KKR & Co Inc.

2.18. WHY DO INVESTORS TYPICALLY USE IRR TO MEASURE PERFORMANCE?

IRR is a popular metric that reports returns in percentage units annually. IRR includes the present value of cash contributed, the present value of distributions, and the estimated value of unrealized (ongoing) investments. However, this measure is overstated since the gross calculation does not include any performance fees earned by the GP. It includes drawdowns and distributions such as capital gains and income through dividends. IRR allows investors to directly compare investments that exhibit irregular timing and size of cash flows. IRR shouldn't be confused with the standard holding period return used to determine public investments' performance. Instead, the IRR calculation evolves as a fund updates projections for future value and as actual returns emerge by the end of the fund's life. Before that point, part of the IRR calculation includes an estimate of unrealized value results. Some refer to this calculation as an interim IRR or a since inception IRR (SI-IRR). Most GPs report a gross IRR in marketing materials, although the actual (lower) return realized by the LPs is a net IRR, reflecting the deduction of all fees.

2.19. WHAT ARE THE PRIMARY ADVANTAGES AND DISADVANTAGES OF USING IRR TO MEASURE A PE'S PERFORMANCE?

Although many investors and analysts use an IRR-based measure to report PE performance, it isn't without criticism. Hence, such a measure has benefits and drawbacks. The primary advantages of using IRR include the following:

- *Ability to handle irregular cash flows.* PE, in general, and VC, in particular, have unconventional cash flow streams. Cash flows are often negative in the first 3–5 years due to paying fees and expenses and not harvesting profits from initial investments. As investments develop, mature, and turn profitable, the timing of the harvesting doesn't occur simultaneously. Harvesting doesn't happen on a predictable schedule and extends for the remainder of the fund's life. However, IRR allows for analyzing irregular cash flows. In turn, IRR enables investors to compare and rank investments, which permit determining the offers with the highest percentage return.

> "I think good private equity investors create a lot more economic value than they destroy."
>
> Bill Ackman

- *Consideration for the time value of money.* Because IRR applies a discount rate associated with cash flows, all else equal, those cash flows occurring earlier in the process carry more weight in the overall return calculation. For example, generating $1,000 today has more value than generating $1,000 next year. IRR explicitly incorporates these differences in its calculations.

- *Ease of calculation.* Investors and analysts can easily calculate IRR using a calculator or software package such as Excel. Once calculated, IRR provides a way to describe the performance as a return, which is a common way of conceptualizing performance.

The primary concerns for using IRR as a return measure for PE include the following:

- *Reinvestment rate assumption.* The IRR calculation assumes reinvesting the cash flows generated throughout the fund's life at the same rate of return. This assumption can lead to misstating actual ex-post performance for a given investment when returns on reinvested capital don't match those produced by the original PE investment.

- *Ineffectiveness in comparing projects.* IRR isn't an effective way of selecting one project over another, known as *mutually exclusive projects.* IRR fails as a comparative metric, because it doesn't consider the scale of the projects. *Scale* refers to the amount of capital required to initiate a project. In particular, IRR fails to compare two projects that require different amounts of capital accurately, but the smaller project has a higher IRR.

- *IRR manipulation due to the timing of distributions.* GPs can manipulate performance based on the timing of project exits. In particular, they can artificially improve IRR performance by changing the timing of distributions to investors. GPs recognizing "early wins" (i.e., those projects offering faster returns of large magnitude) and delaying the recognition of "late losses" (i.e., those projects that ultimately underperform) creates a higher IRR calculation.

- *Multiple IRRs.* IRR represents the discount rate at which the present value of all cash flows equals zero (breaks even). Mathematically, a project can generate multiple IRRs. In particular, if a fund generates more than one sign change (e.g., a negative cash flow followed by a positive cash flow) in cash flows across years, return calculations may result in more than one IRR calculation. Often none of the calculated IRRs reflects the actual IRR.

- *Misleading progression of performance over a fund's life.* To compute IRR, realized returns are combined with projected future returns to create an evolving IRR measure previously identified as an interim IRR or a SI-IRR. You should interpret these interim calculations with caution as a given point-in-time estimate may result in a misleading assessment. A fund that generates early wins with an assumed potential for future success can produce an overly optimistic performance assessment. However, as the fund matures, the interim IRR calculation starts to converge to the ultimate final IRR, which can paint an entirely different picture across time.

- *Accounting for incentive fees.* The IRR provides a snapshot of fund performance, but it doesn't consider the actual net return earned by LPs. In other words, IRR doesn't account for the actual management fees or the timing of the fees. As such, LPs have to make assumptions about the magnitude and timing of fees to adjust how a fund's IRR performance is likely to result in actual returns to them.

2.20. WHAT OTHER MEASURES CAN INVESTORS USE TO ASSESS PE PERFORMANCE?

Although IRR is the most commonly used measure for PE performance, it has shortcomings, as already noted. Several other measures are also available. Some offer potential fixes to IRR problems, but they have drawbacks.

- *Modified IRR (MIRR)*. One criticism of the IRR method is its reinvestment rate assumption that projects can reinvest their cash flows at the same rate earned. MIRR removes the assumption of reinvesting cash flows at the same rate. Instead, MIRR assumes a reinvestment rate, separate from the project's rate of return. MIRR calculates returns by considering all of a project's cash flows based on the time value of money. As a result, MIRR provides a better way to account for what happens with cash flows once received, reflecting an investment's true profitability. The primary issue with MIRR is the assigned of the reinvestment rate. Often, investors use a proxy for the cost of capital, which itself is subjective.

- *Multiples of invested capital (MIC)*. MIC provides a cash-on-cash measure of how much return investors receive relative to their investment. Many in the PE industry use multiples, because they offer an easy way to show the scale of the investment returns. Calculating MICs involves dividing the value of the returns by the amount of money invested. IRR-based measures provide practical ways of presenting an investment's returns, but don't offer information on returns based on scale without having explicit details on how long the fund is likely to exist. In contrast, multiples provide an efficient way to show returns to scale. Funds commonly report two MICs: distribution to paid-in capital (DPI) and TVPI capital, which differ in whether they include residual values.

  o *DPI*. DPI measures the ratio of money distributed to date by a fund against the total amount of money paid into the fund. As a fund draws down funds without harvesting returns, DPI is zero but increases as distributions occur. If DPI increases to a value of 1, the fund has broken even, as money paid in is equal to money distributed. Values above 1 indicate that the fund has paid out more than invested.

o *TVPI capital.* TVPI measures a PE's overall performance with a ratio of the fund's cumulative distributions and residual value to the paid-in capital. TVPI includes the investment's multiple assuming the sale of the unrealized assets at current valuations. This estimate, known as *residual value*, is added to distributions already received. Although TVPI may suggest a fuller picture of a fund's returns, the valuation method used for the remaining investments requiring harvesting affects the residual value.

For TVPI and DPI to reflect an actual return metric requires presenting them on a net basis after removing GP total fees. DPI provides a clear metric of the actual multiple of cash invested received by an investor but lacks a comprehensive view of the actual return, because it excludes unharvested investments. TVPI provides a more comprehensive metric that accounts for potential returns based on a residual estimate, but it introduces a subjective element into the return calculation. Given this difference, LPs prefer TVPI during the earlier part of a fund's life but DPI toward the end of its life. Although MICs are useful in exploring returns based on investment, they ignore the time value of money. For example, a higher TVPI multiple reliant on the potential for late fund harvesting is less valuable to an LP than a comparable multiple generated based on previous distributions. Additionally, MICs may not provide critical information on a project's scale or the absolute returns' size. Thus, using MICs for evaluating mutually exclusive projects isn't practical.

• *PME.* PME is a return measure that allows investors to compare an IRR-based measure to the public market performance that would have been generated over the same period. Calculating a PME involves developing a hypothetical investment vehicle, in which purchases and harvests in the public market index mimic a fund's irregular cash flows. As with the previous discussion on performance measures, net cash flows to date provide the most convincing returns for funds. Using indices to reflect a proxy for reinvestment potential offers the most appropriate return comparison between private and public investments. Private and public equity have the same cash flows over time, but different end values, giving two directly comparable IRRs. Selecting a PE index to establish a comparative network introduces subjectivity, which can produce misleading results. In general, PME is most effective when assessing more mature investments, in which the residual value is a smaller fraction of the cash flow projects. PME is inappropriate if the PE market returns are negative. In which case, the PE portfolio is being compared against a short position in the public market. Additionally, PME doesn't account for a project's scale and can encounter issues with abnormal cash flows.

2.21. WHY IS MANAGER SELECTION A CRITICAL CONSIDERATION IN PE INVESTING?

PE manager selection is critical for two primary reasons. First, the distribution of PE returns exhibits much more variation than that of public equity returns. Because the best perform-ing PE GPs outperform the best performing public equity managers, accessing the best performing PE GPs can add considerable value. Conversely, the worst-performing PE GPs underperform the worst-performing public equity managers. Some evidence exists for performance persistence among PE managers, and something infrequently observed with public equity managers. Some attribute performance persistence to the GP's ability to build on a network for deal flow, organizational capabilities, specialized knowledge of sectors, and the ability to create value through generating enhanced operational efficiencies of companies. Academic evidence pre-2000 universally recognized performance persistence as a fact. However, more recent studies offer weakened support for persistence among VC funds, especially among the top-performing buyout funds.

Identifying portfolio persistence is challenging for several reasons. For example, researchers have different definitions of what constitutes top performance. Size bias exists in studies on this subject. Research is unable to identify secular market trends in studies. Finally, differences exist in sector performance. Still, evidence of performance persistence merits consideration for manager selection. However, gaining access to top managers is challenging because of oversubscription to their funds resulting from demand, loyal following of current LPs on follow-up funds, and preference for returning investors by GPs.

2.22. WHAT FACTORS ARE RELEVANT TO CONSIDER IN SELECTING A PE MANAGER?

You should consider several factors when selecting a PE manager, including the following:

- *Desired exposure.* A potential PE investor should develop a "wish list" based on the type of exposure desired. Classifying candidate funds based on past or potential future performance provides a target list.

- *Diversification.* Diversifying across funds can reduce the overall risk of PE exposure. Those investors gaining exposure through PIVs are likely to find that funds seek to diversify based on stage focus, vintage year, sector, and style. Diversification across PE funds is effective in risk reduction. For VC, investors can reduce about 80% of the standard deviation and skewness with 20 to 30 funds.

- *Due diligence.* Investors in PE must engage in appropriate due diligence to ensure that the exposure they are gaining is consistent with the rest of their portfolio. This due diligence should consider both investment and operational due diligence.

  o *Investment assessment.* PE funds face market risk based on valuation uncertainty and liquidity risk because of the discounts applied to PE due to a lack of an active secondary market. Financial risk incorporates both market and liquidity risk. These two risks show a high correlation during financial crises. PE also has commitment risk because of the unpredictability of returns and the possibility of not generating a return to cover invested capital.

  o *Operational risk assessment.* Operational risk assessment is essential due to the long-term nature of PE investments. Investors need to have a general understanding of back-office procedures, the ability for systems to be scalable with sufficient personnel, and an assurance that the management team can adapt to external changes. They also need to understand a fund's technology and cash management processes and be comfortable with risk management processes.

2.23. WHAT ARE DEBT INSTRUMENTS RELATED TO PE?

VC and buyouts are the most well-known forms of PE. Both are forms of equity financing. PE also has several debt forms of investment.

- *Mezzanine debt. Mezzanine debt* is a hybrid of debt and equity. Two of the more common types of mezzanine debt are *convertible bonds* and *subordinated bonds with warrants*. These securities are similar in that they both enable debt holders to gain equity exposure. For convertible bonds, seizing such an opportunity means the holder loses the debt exposure by converting the bond into a stated number of equity shares. With subordinated bonds issued with the warrants, the holder retains the debt ownership and gains equity exposure by exercising the warrants, a type of option, to buy a fixed number of shares at a stated fixed price over a stated time frame.

  o *Convertible bonds.* A convertible bond is a fixed-income corporate debt security allowing holders to convert into a predetermined number of shares.

  o *Subordinated bonds with warrants.* By its nature, mezzanine debt holds the lowest priority in the pecking order of debt financing. As a result, mezzanine debt commands a risk premium for its subordinated position. To "sweeten" the offering, companies may choose to issue warrants.

- *Distressed debt. Distressed debt* involves investing in companies in or near default. Three motives underly such investment.

  o *Conversion of debt to equity.* Distressed debt investors could want an opportunity to take control by converting debt to equity as a part of bankruptcy negotiations. In the

> *"A good default, like Portugal or Greece, would be very good for the private equity business."*
> David Bonderman

United States, companies filing Chapter 11 bankruptcy wish to remain a going concern. Bondholders negotiate the terms of a capital structure overhaul to avoid involving a bankruptcy court. As a part of the negotiations, distressed debt investors seek opportunities for equity representation in the reorganization. Additionally, they often demand board representation.

o *Active investing*. Distressed debt investors may choose to take an active role but not to acquire control. For this group, they may pursue debt conversion to equity.

o *Passive investing*. Distressed debt investors may seek a passive strategy. They may believe that a company's position is likely to improve or hedge such improvement by taking a short position in its stock to benefit from possible improvements or further deterioration.

2.24. WHAT ROLE DOES MEZZANINE DEBT PLAY FOR THE ISSUING COMPANY?

Mezzanine debt represents flexibility in financing firm operations. Unlike other debt obligations, a company with mezzanine debt has no obligation to make interest payments. In other words, suspending interest payments doesn't send the company into bankruptcy. Issues are typically between 4 and 6 years. They often have a bullet payment of principal, which allows investors to receive a larger payment at the end of the issue's life to forgo regular interest payments. Interest payments can be either in the form of cash or an in-kind distribution, including equity "kickers," in which holders can earn shares of stock.

Issuers use mezzanine financing for different reasons, including engaging in management buyouts, fund growth or expansion, acquiring companies, recapitalizing a firm, engaging in commercial real estate financing, participating in LBOs, or meeting bridge financing needs. Issuing mezzanine debt often lowers a company's cost of capital. Since mezzanine debt is above equity in the capital structure pecking order, it has a lower required return, which results in less expensive financing.

2.25. WHAT ARE SOME RECENT TRENDS AND INNOVATIONS IN PE INVESTING?

PE is a rapidly evolving investment option, as indicated by the following three noteworthy trends.

- *Developing a secondary market.* Historically, the lack of a secondary market locked in PE investors for the PE fund's life. Thus, the lack of liquidity associated with PE investments allowed the GP to commit to long-term strategies without concern for LP withdrawals. As such, LPs received a premium for the fund's lack of liquidity. If LPs wanted to exit the investment prematurely, they had to seek permission from the GP based on the LPA and find a third party willing to step in to transfer ownership. As a result, LPs took deep discounts to the implied PE value to exit.

  Since the early 2000s, a fledgling PE secondary market emerged and grown steadily. A more structured format now exists for enabling original LPs to sell their ownership units for a market-determined purchase price with the GP's consent. The price in the secondary market price is typically a percentage of the published PE fund's NAV. The buyer and seller agree on the valuation or reference date at the start of the transaction, known as the *NAV valuation date*. The seller receives reimbursement for post-reference date capital calls, and post-reference date distributions reduce the purchase price. Secondary market transactions typically occur between 3 and 5 years after the primary fundraising occurs. Through secondary market transactions, the conversion rate has dramatically increased with deals worth more than $80 billion completed during 2019.

Secondary markets offer several benefits, including: (1) enhanced visibility on portfolio companies as underperforming investments are typically already written down by the point of secondary transactions, (2) shallower and shorter J-curve effect as secondary markets avoid a fund's initial fee load, (3) greater access for LPs who previously could not gain entrance to a GP, and (4) lower loss rates. The J-curve is shallower, because the secondary transaction occurs after most initial upfront spending has taken place. The J-curve is shorter since the secondary transition typically occurs near the PE fund's life's mid-point.

- *Convergence of hedge funds and PE.* Historically, hedge funds specialized in short-term trading strategies, while PE targeted long-term strategies in private companies in which they attempted to improve their financial and operational performance. Since the early 2000s, the lines between hedge funds and PE have increasingly blurred. Several reasons help to explain this trend:

  o *Increased institutionalization of hedge funds.* Hedge funds outnumber PE funds threefold and manage at least five times more capital. With this growth of hedge funds, greater institutionalization has occurred with hedge funds featuring large research staffs and extensive industry experience, which they can bring to the PE markets.

  o *Reduced   arbitrage   opportunities.*   Greater institutionalization is further encouraged, because hedge funds are finding fewer arbitrage opportunities in increasingly more efficient markets. Thus, hedge funds seek opportunities in less traditional markets, including those historically targeted by PE firms.

o *Shift to auction markets.* The PE market has also matured with a shift from propriety deal flow to a more auction-based market for buyout opportunities. The increased use of auction markets, along with their increased transparency, has opened the possibilities for hedge funds to gain access to markets that were previously the domain of PE funds.

- *Private investment in public equities (PIPE).* PIPE is the process of a PE firm buying stock directly from a public company, often at a discount. Companies find this option attractive as PIPEs have fewer regulatory requirements, saving time and money for issuing companies. However, such shares are unavailable on a stock exchange but take place only in the private placement market. Most PIPE agreements allow investors to buy securities to convert into common stock at a predetermined price or exchange rate. PE funds often seek out investments in public companies as a part of a capital restructuring strategy to enhance returns. The increased participation of PE firms is threefold: (1) as a response to the limited credit availability for the leveraged transactions they typically pursue, (2) lower valuations with issues giving them terms more in line with private transactions, and (3) additional covenants in the purchase agreements that provide PE firms mode information and corporate governance rights.

2.26. WHAT ARE SOME ONLINE RESOURCES FOR PE?

Various online resources are available for PE.

- *SEC* (https://www.investor.gov/introduction-investing/basics/investment-products/private-equity-funds) explains PE and factors to consider before investing.

- *Motley Fool* (https://www.fool.com/investing/2017/10/07/how-to-invest-in-private-equity.aspx) provides useful information on how to invest in PE.

- *Eurekahedge* (http://www.eurekahedge.com/Research/News/886/Investing_in_Private_Equities_through_a_Fund_of_Funds) discusses how to invest in PE through a fund of funds.

TAKEAWAYS

By offering investors an opportunity to add exposures not traded publicly, PE could increase their portfolio returns while lowering risk. Thus, savvy investors should be aware of this chapter's key takeaways.

- Determine how PE may fit into your portfolio.

- Review the PE fund with a financial advisor's help to ensure that it is suitable for your investment objectives and time horizon.

- Recall that VC is riskier than buyout funds but potentially offers more generous rewards.

- Be aware that the easiest way to get into PE investing is to buy shares of an appropriate ETF or fund of funds.

- Consider PE's risk-return tradeoffs before making any decision.

- Understand the costs associated with investing in PE funds.

- Realize that LPs are committed to their investment for 7–10 years and that its secondary market is growing but remains relatively small.

- Measure the performance of PE using IRR.

3

INVESTING IN REAL ESTATE: IT'S NOT JUST YOUR HOME

"The best investment on earth is earth."

Louis Glickman

Real estate is a tangible asset that is familiar but often misunderstood at the same time. You may think of real estate as the place where you grew up. Whether your family owned or rented the residence, it was your home. Unlike the other alternative assets discussed in this book, you need real estate as a shelter and a place to stay warm and safe. Without a roof over your head, you're in a situation in which daily life becomes a struggle. Thinking about investing in other investments is unlikely to be a priority if you don't have a place to live.

Is real estate an investment? Real estate consists of at least two major types: residential and commercial. *Residential real estate* includes single-family homes, two-family homes, and apartment buildings. The residential real estate market includes your home, so it's not an investment in the traditional sense, although it may appreciate over time. However, given the homeownership costs in some markets, not viewing your home as an investment or part of your investment portfolio is tricky. At a minimum, homeownership is a commitment to repay the mortgage, maintain the property, and pay taxes. A *mortgage* is a loan to purchase real estate, where the property serves as collateral for the loan. Conversely, *commercial real estate* is the type of real estate that generates income primar-ily through rent. It includes office buildings, shopping malls, and apartment build-ings. You may be less familiar with some others like storage facilities, warehouses, and industrial properties.

> *"The major fortunes in America have been made in land."*
> John D. Rockefeller

This chapter focuses on how you can invest in real estate. Fortunately, financial markets allow you to invest in real estate directly by buying a property or indirectly through a pooled investment vehicle (PIV). A PIV may sound familiar, especially if you're aware of mutual funds and exchange-traded funds (ETFs), which are examples of PIVs. Opportu-nities are also available to invest in real estate as an owner (through equity) or as a lender (through debt). So, you can see that perhaps investing in real estate is probably easier than you thought.

Anecdotally, real estate makes for some fascinating and profitable stories. For example, consider perhaps the best real estate investment in history. In 1626, Peter Minuet of the Dutch West India Company bought the island of Man-hattan from the local Native American tribe for the often-quoted $24. Although the details may be inaccurate, it's still an instructive story. The Dutch thought they bought the land, but the Native Americans didn't have a concept of land ownership.

> *"He is not a full man who does not own a piece of land."*
> Hebrew Proverb

They believed that people couldn't trade water, air, and land, because they are shared resources. Communication and understanding are critical to real estate transactions even today. At the time, the locals thought they received the better end of the deal since they may have received useful tools and similar items and didn't give up "owner-

> "If you don't own a home, buy one. If you own a home, buy another one. If you own two homes, buy a third. And, lend your relatives the money to buy a home."
>
> John Paulson

ship." Ultimately, conflict ensued over this misunderstanding, and the Dutch West India Company suspended Minuet from his post. Today, Manhattan real estate is worth close to $2 trillion, or about Canada's annual gross domestic product.

Previous chapters discussed hedge funds and private equity as investments for qualified investors. Real estate doesn't have that barrier. One aspect of the quintessential "American Dream" is homeownership, which the government encourages and even subsidizes primarily through tax incentives. However, many other real estate related investments are available. These investments are the focus of this chapter.

3.1. WHAT IS REAL ESTATE AND ITS MAJOR CHARACTERISTICS?

Real estate refers to land and any structures on it. The land can be vacant or developed. Other names for real estate that includes natural resources, crops, or livestock are farmland and timberland. Real estate is inherently an illiquid asset. You can't move it from one location to another, but you can modify it for your specific use, subject to local ordinances and regulations. Real estate has public and private markets and equity and debt markets and consists of direct and indirect investments. Unlike in active equity markets, no one universally agreed upon "value" exists for real estate since properties trade infrequently. Each piece of real estate is unique. Even two apartments with the same dimensions in the same building have different views, modifications, and wear and tear. These features differ from other investments, such as a stock or bond, in which your share is the same as another's share and each party is entitled to equal proportionate claims on the investment.

3.2. WHAT ARE THE PRIMARY PROPERTY TYPES?

Many different property types are available, and their definitions often vary. You're most likely familiar with single-family, residential real estate. Although it typically includes a single-family home, residential real estate also includes two-family homes and small (usually up to four units) apartment buildings. Some properties are mixed-use, in which the lower level is a storefront or business, and the upper units are apartments or residences. Other types of multi-family dwellings include large apartment buildings, condominiums (ownership of the unit and shared ownership of common areas), and apartment communities.

The other major property type is commercial. Commercial property's main features are that you can't live there, and it's intended to generate income. Brief descriptions of various kinds of commercial property follow.

- *Retail* – usage for shopping and direct customer contact. This type of commercial property includes strip malls, regional malls, and shopping centers.

- *Industrial* – manufacturing facilities and production of physical products. Subdivisions include warehousing, heavy manufacturing, and light manufacturing.

> *"Owning a home is a keystone of wealth... both financial affluence and emotional security."*
> Suze Orman

- *Office* – leasing of property for business services. This category consists of Class A, B, and C. Class A properties are the best in terms of location and construction; Class B properties have quality locations or construction; Class C properties are outdated and in a poor location.

- *Hospitality* – includes full-service hotels in the central business district, boutique hotels, and extended stay hotels.

- *Land* – raw land, undeveloped farm, or pasture land is considered greenfield. Brownfield land may have environmental issues or previous commercial usage. A *brownfield investment* improves upon existing real estate, while a *greenfield investment* relates to the land in its more natural condition.

- *Mixed-use* – any combination of the property types mentioned but usually involves retail/restaurant below and living space above.

3.3. WHAT ARE THE ADVANTAGES OF OWNING REAL ESTATE?

Real estate provides several advantages to investors, including stable cash flows, capital appreciation, tax advantages, inflation protection, and diversification. It's also possible to leverage real estate to build wealth. Here are some of these advantages.

- *Predictable cash flows.* Rental income from owning a rental property is the primary source of cash flow for any real estate asset. Whether the property is commercial, office building, or multi-unit residential property, rental income is generally a stable cash flow. Although situations occur where tenants may be unable to pay their rent due to shocks to the economic environment, such as the COVID-19 pandemic, these situations are uncommon. Further, rents tend to rise in times of inflation, acting as a partial hedge against inflation.

- *Capital appreciation.* Property values (prices) are subject to change, much like in the equity markets. However, unlike stocks, real estate is generally less volatile, making it a relatively less risky asset. An advantage of property ownership, aside from rental income, is the potential for that property to increase in value, adding to the potential return an investor may receive.

- *Tax advantages.* Many tax advantages are available to owners of income-generating properties that are generally associated with the cost of owning, operating, and managing properties. For example, real estate owners can deduct the depreciation of the property value from their taxes. They can also depreciate expenses associated with increasing the property's value over its useful lifespan. Such depreciation potentially

> *"Real estate is an imperishable asset, ever increasing in value. It is the most solid security that human ingenuity has devised. It is the basis for all security and about the only indestructible security."*
>
> Russell Sage

allows investors to benefit from deductions for literally decades. Further deductions come from mortgage interest expense deductions, deferral of capital gains taxes via a 1031 exchange, property tax deductions, and so on. Under Section 1031 of the US Internal Revenue Code, a taxpayer may defer

> *"I have always liked real estate; farm land, pasture land, timber land and city property. I have had experience with all of them. I guess I just naturally like "the good Earth," the foundation of all our wealth."*
>
> Jesse Jones

recognizing capital gains and related federal income tax liability when exchanging certain property types. In short, if you invest in real estate, you should be aware of the current tax laws associated with such investments.

* *Diversification.* Real estate generally exhibits a low or possibly negative correlation with other asset classes. Therefore, allocating a portion of a portfolio to real estate allows you to better manage your risk exposure across various asset classes by decreasing the portfolio's volatility and aggregate risk.

3.4. WHAT ARE THE CHALLENGES AND RISKS TO REAL ESTATE OWNERSHIP?

Real estate, like all investments, has its own set of risks and rewards. Before jumping into a real estate investment, you need to be aware of the possible risks.

> *"Buying real estate is not only the best way, the quickest way, the safest way, but the only way to become wealthy."*
>
> Marshall Field

- *Market risk.* *Market risk* refers to the systematic risk that may cause a loss of value due to external risk factors. For example, general economic conditions could reduce consumer demand, causing retail locations to perform poorly, generating insufficient revenue, and impairing their ability to pay rent. As a result, property valuations suffer. You can partly mitigate market risk through geographic and property type diversification.

- *Asset and idiosyncratic risk.* *Asset risk* refers to the general risk exposures shared by the entire real estate asset class. These exposures may arise from a macroeconomic event that adversely affects property values or a shock to funding markets that affect mortgage rates. *Idiosyncratic risk* is associated with shocks that may affect a specific type of real estate, individual property, or region. For instance, industrial and commercial properties may be more sensitive to demand for consumer goods. In contrast, an office building rented by a bank would be less sensitive to shifts in demand. Idiosyncratic risk relates to a microcosm of adverse effects rather than a macro-level exposure.

- Liquidity risk. *Liquidity* refers to the speed and ease of converting an asset into cash. For instance, publicly-traded stocks are generally highly liquid because investors can enter and exit positions with ease in the open market. Bank deposits are another example of a highly liquid asset as they're almost as good as cash. Because real estate can be one of the most illiquid assets you can own, you need to understand the risks involved in locking up your capital in a real estate property when deciding where and when to invest. Could you use that capital to achieve a better yield elsewhere? Are you willing to lock up money for multiple years? How soon and how certain are you that you can sell the property later? These types of questions arise when examining the liquidity risk of real estate ownership. Thus, you need to develop several exit strategies before investing if the investment performs adversely or you want to free up capital to invest elsewhere.

• *Property-specific risk.* Managing a property is arguably the most hands-on and intensive aspect of owning real estate. When something breaks or a tenant is unhappy, the property owner needs to address these issues quickly and effectively. Otherwise, tenants may leave, increasing the vacancy rate and severely affecting the investment's cash flow profile. To avoid dealing with these issues themselves, many property owners either use a management company or hire a property manager. Maintenance and property management, while necessary, can increase the costs of owning a property.

3.5. WHAT WAYS ARE AVAILABLE TO INVEST IN REAL ESTATE?

Real estate investing can be broadly summarized by the real estate matrix in Table 3.1, showing the four combinations of public or private investments in debt or equity.

A *real estate investment trust* (REIT) is a particular type of real estate investment described further in the next section. A REIT is essentially a PIV in which investors contribute capital to buy real estate. Professional managers operate REITs, which trade on public markets. The equity part of the name means proportionate ownership known as an equity REIT (eREIT). The largest eREIT is Simon Property Group (NYSE: SPG), which

> *"But land is land, and it's safer than the stocks and bonds of Wall Street swindlers."*
> Eugene O'Neill

Table 3.1   The Real Estate Investment Matrix

	Public	Private
Equity	Equity REITs Real Estate Operating Companies	Direct ownership (landlord)
Debt	Mortgage REITs Real estate securities (MBS and CMBS)	A lender in the real estate transaction

Note: The table displays the public/private and debt/equity investments in real estate.

owns shopping malls and outlet centers. Mortgage REITs (mREITs) also pool investor capital but invest in the securities related to the real estate. For example, an mREIT invests in the debt issued by the pool itself but not the actual property. Question 6 discusses eREITs and mREITs in more detail.

Direct equity ownership occurs when the investor is the traditional landlord. You buy the building, usually with a mortgage, and actively manage the property. Direct equity ownership spans small rental units for individuals to large *trophy properties*, including high-profile or landmark buildings. For example, RXR Realty owns 75 Rockefeller Plaza in New York City. This form of investing provides the purest access to the real estate market but is also the riskiest.

Be wary of the advice to invest your excess cash in rental properties, especially residential real estate, because it's often a terrible idea for several reasons. For instance, income isn't guaranteed and generating a compelling return can be difficult. Such "hands-on" investing offers less diversification than with an eREIT. Thus, you bear the risk associated with the property with little diversification. To diversify the real estate investment, an investor would need to buy other properties, often at a substantial cost. Additionally, real estate is illiquid, so you can't necessarily sell it when you want. This type of stable properties that don't require much maintenance or have predicable cost structures and are occupied by creditworthy tenants on long-term leases. For example, the office building for a large insurance company with a 30-year lease illustrates a core investment, because the firm is unlikely to break its lease but is likely to have cash on hand to pay rent. However, using leverage and aggressive financing structures could alter a core property's profile, because different financing structures could fundamentally change an investment's risk profile, but not necessarily the property itself.

Core-plus. Core-plus investment strategies tend to have higher risk profiles than core but still exhibit relatively stable and robust cash flows. These properties have a greater potential for growth through property improvements that increase management efficiency or replacing tenants. Although core-plus properties are still stable investments, they exhibit a higher probability of cash flow shortfalls or value depreciation than core investments.

> "I would give a thousand furlongs of sea for an acre of barren ground."
> William Shakespeare

Value-add. Value-add strategies are like growth equity strategies, such as investing in a young, fast-growing tech startup with low or negative cash flow but considerable upside potential. These properties generally have riskier profiles and unstable or undesirable cash flow profiles at purchase. Yet, after addressing operational issues and efficiency improvements, such properties have much higher upside potential than core or core-plus. They're also much more hands-on than the core and core-plus strategies.

direct equity ownership is difficult for small investors but easy for pension funds, life insurance companies, and similar institutional investors.

Opportunities are also available to serve as the bank in a real estate transaction. The investor would lend funds to a borrower who purchases real estate. The property serves as collateral for the loan so that if the borrower defaults, the lender has recourse on the property. *Recourse* means that the lender has the legal right to seize the property in default.

3.6. WHAT IS A REIT AND ITS MAJOR TYPES?

In general, a REIT is a pooled investment in real estate through outright ownership, operation, or financing. REITs have a unique structure granted by Congress as part of the Cigar Excise Act Extension in 1960 to promote real estate investing for investors both large and small. Since REITs trade as stocks, they create liquidity in a market that is inherently illiquid. Additionally, investors can access diversified real estate portfolios with a relatively small initial investment.

Four major types of REITs are available: eREITs, mREITs, public non-listed REITs (PLNRs), and private REITs. Some discussion of each type occurs below, but most of the emphasis is on eREITs because they're the largest and most influential segment.

• *Equity REITs.* REITs, particularly eREITs, are flexible investments because you can buy shares of a REIT just as you would any other stock. Similarly, you can take a long or short position. A *long position* is when you buy the REIT anticipating a price increase, while a *short position* profits from a price decrease. You can also gain exposure to REITs through a mutual fund or an ETF. US exchange-traded REITs own about 500,000 properties with an aggregate market value of $2 trillion. REITs earn profits by owning or leasing real estate, collecting the rent, and distributing profits as dividends to shareholders.

- *Mortgage REITs.* mREITs finance purchases of mortgages and mortgage-backed securities (MBS) with debt and equity capital. Their goal is to profit from the net interest margin between the financing costs and the mortgage assets' investment returns. mREITs also buy MBS and receive the cash flows directly from the MBS that is passed-through from the original borrowers net of fees. Therefore, mREITs provide liquidity and funding for residential and income-producing real estate.

An MBS pools mortgages and distributes specific cash flows to different investor classes called *tranches*. Figure 3.1 provides a simplified picture summarizing the MBS structure. Assets, also known as *collateral*, transfer their cash flows into

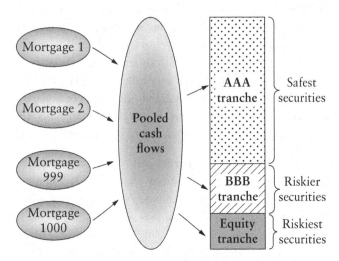

Figure 3.1.   Basic Structure of a Mortgage-Backed Security

Note: This figure illustrates the process of creating an MBS and tranching of cash flows.

the pool. The pool distributes the cash flows to tranches based on prespecified rules. In this illus of the cash flows go to the senior (safest) AAA tra the BBB tranche, and the residual, if any, to the e

- *PLNRs.* These securities must register with the Exchange Commission (SEC) but don't trade stock exchanges. They're virtually identica traded REITs but impose restrictions on red lock-up periods. Therefore, investors must the liquidity of PLNRs is much lower than p REITs and mREITs. Minimum investment si between $1,000 and $2,500, an amount w many smaller investors.

- *Private REITs.* The shares of private REITs a with the SEC, don't trade on a national s and are restricted to accredited investoi institutional buyers. Chapter 1 includes an accredited investor. The minimum i is generally between $1,000 and $25,(investments are private, no public source performance data of private REITs.

3.7. WHAT ARE THE DIFFERENT IN STRATEGIES – CORE, CORE-PLUS, V OPPORTUNISTIC?

Real estate investors may follow any of the fol

- *Core.* Core real estate investment strat to income or dividend strategies in investments generate steady income by risk properties. This strategy generally

- *Opportunistic.* Of all the strategies, opportunistic real estate strategies exhibit much more risk and are akin to distressed investing in the equity and credit markets. These properties generally require the most attention and improvements before realizing any returns.

> *"Before you start trying to work out which direction the property market is headed, you should be aware that there are markets within markets."*
> Paul Clitheroe

Investors often don't receive returns until at least three years after the initial investment. This strategy usually requires experience to turnaround the property. For example, the acquisition team may completely rebuild a property or redevelop the land. This strategy carries the greatest risk profile and potential for return.

3.8. WHAT ARE THE CRITICAL FEATURES OF REITS?

REITs have some technical restrictions, such as the "5–50" rule, in which the five largest shareholders can't exceed 50% of the total ownership. REITs must also invest at least 75% of their total assets in real estate, and at least 75% of gross income must relate to real estate. REITs' most attractive feature is that they can "pass-through" their earnings untaxed as dividends to shareholders. This tax feature applies as long as a REIT declares dividends of at least 90% of its taxable earnings. This pass-through feature benefits the REIT by avoiding taxes and shareholders who aren't faced with double taxation on the dividends received. A downside is that REITs may have more variable dividends than other companies and retain smaller cash balances. However, both the cash flows and dividends associated with REITs are reasonably stable.

3.9. WHAT APPROACHES CAN INVESTORS USE TO VALUE REAL ESTATE PROPERTY?

Investors use different valuation methods depending on their specialization and market type. They generally use several standard methods for an investor looking to generate income from the property. These methods are of little value for either personal-use or residential buyers.

- *Direct capitalization.* The direct capitalization method of real estate valuation divides the income generated from the property, known as the *net operating income* (NOI), by the capitalization rate over that same period as shown in Equation (3.1),

> "Buy land, they are not making it anymore."
> Mark Twain

$$\text{Property value} = \frac{\text{NOI}}{\text{Cap Rate}}. \qquad (3.1)$$

The *capitalization rate* (cap rate) is a proxy measure of the expected rate of return an investor may earn on a property. This rate is determined by dividing the NOI by the property's asset value, which can be determined by appraisal, market value, or similar properties. One caveat involving the cap rate and valuation methods is that they use historical data and assumptions made by the analyst or investor. Because market dynamics change, no guarantee exists that these valuation methods produce an accurate measure of value. Thus, they're only as good as the data and analytical methods used to calculate them.

- *Discounted cash flow (DCF).* DCF analysis is a flexible method used by investors to value any cash flow generating asset, including equities, loans, and real estate. Equation (3.2) shows the basic DCF equation:

$$\text{DCF valuation} = \frac{CF_1}{(1+r)^1} + \frac{CF_2}{(1+r)^2} + \frac{CF_3}{(1+r)^3}$$
$$+ \cdots \frac{CF_n + \text{Terminal Value}}{(1+r)^n}, \tag{3.2}$$

where $CF_1 \ldots CF_n$ are the cash flows projected out to period n, r is the discount rate, and the terminal value is the property's final expected value or horizon price. The *horizon price* is the expected price of a future sale. In real estate investing, the *discount rate* typically represents an investment's expected rate of return and can be estimated from comparable properties in the area.

This method is time-consuming and computationally expensive for an investor, because it entails formalizing specific expectations for each similar property's NOI and terminal value. As such, investors use a proxy measure by adding a premium, which incorporates both a risk and liquidity premium, to the risk-free rate, represented by a US Treasury bill or some other comparable security. Other methods of determining the discount rate are available, which include using investor surveys and analyzing historical returns. However, other more advanced techniques are available for aggregating the necessary data required to create a more statistically sound estimate of the discount. As with any valuation method, the DCF method is an estimate and often relies on assumptions of market conditions. Valuation models are fluid and their assumptions change along with the markets to reflect a more accurate picture of value.

- *Comparable sales.* The comparable sales method involves a direct extrapolation of value by analyzing the sales data of similar properties. Investors can use this method as a reality

> *"Land monopoly is not only monopoly, but it is by far the greatest of monopolies; it is a perpetual monopoly, and it is the mother of all other forms of monopoly."*
> Winston Churchill

check for other models. It also allows for some insight into the broader market dynamics of the area. Real estate is unique because different geographical localities can exhibit diverse market dynamics, which are generally not the case for other asset classes such as public equities within the same country. The comparable sales method enables investors to check their models' assumptions and determine whether market prices are behaving in a "rational" way, prompting them to either update their models/assumptions or dive more deeply into the dynamics of a local market.

- *Estimating income and caveats of valuation.* Determining value using the direct capitalization (based on forecasted NOI) and DCF methods requires projecting or estimating future cash flows. Although investors can estimate NOI in various ways, they generally use market data obtained via comparable properties in the area. Such data include rental rates, collection loss rates, vacancy rates, average operating

> *"Real estate investing, even on a very small scale, remains a tried and true means of building an individual's cash flow and wealth."*
> Robert Kiyosaki

expenses (e.g., repair, maintenance, and tax costs), market growth rates, and financing costs. Using these data involves several caveats. For example, understanding the effect of vacancy rates on appraisals is essential when analyzing comparable property/market data. Property developers attempt to operate at some desirable occupancy level, which often isn't at the full occupancy rate. An understated (overstated) vacancy rate overstates (understates) a property's NOI, which can substantially affect its valuation.

Another caveat is to understand the effects that differing demand has on rental rates. Demand levels can differ for an area or property due to various phenomena such as seasonality and a change in consumer sentiment, thus affecting rental rates. Investors need to have a sound method of forecasting or measuring this potential impact and incorporating these effects into a valuation.

DCF analysis can much better capture this notion of variability. It allows for projecting cash flows, which can change based on different variables such as vacancy and rental rates. An advantage of using multiple valuation methods is that their results are likely to be more credible if they are similar.

3.10. WHAT ARE SOME TYPICAL REAL ESTATE INDICES?

Many indices are available to track real estate markets and sectors, from global indices to emerging markets to even indices tracking lending rates. Below are a few of the most common indices used to track commercial real estate:

- Dow Jones US Real Estate Index – REITs and other related companies;

- BofA Merrill Lynch US Real Estate Index;

- S&P US Property Index;

- S&P US REIT Index;

- MSCI Core Real Estate Factor Indexes;

- MSCI Liquid Real Estate Indexes;

- MSCI All Equity REITs Index;

- AlphaShares Emerging Markets Real Estate Index;

- FTSE NAREIT Mortgage REITs Index; and

- SCTR Real Estate Sector Indices.

Commercial properties and related activities are the basis for these indices, because they mostly track eREITS and mREITs.

Indices for residential housing are more challenging. The Case-Shiller index uses actual transaction prices, not estimates from appraisals. It traces each sale in the current period back to its purchase to determine an annualized return. Thus, each property used has at least two actual transaction prices. This approach captures real estate appreciation between the two periods. It excludes properties with substantial construction or modification, because the selling price captures factors other than real estate appreciation. Finally, the Case-Shiller index is based on cities or geographic regions and isn't aggregated at the country level.

3.11. HOW DOES DIRECT REAL ESTATE INVESTING DIFFER FROM OWNING SHARES IN A REIT?

Direct investment in real estate and owning shares in a REIT each have pros and cons. Although direct property investment allows investors to gain exposure to local, microstructural growth factors that may be unavailable on the macro level, the lack of data and information on potential properties may be limited compared to data provided by REITs. The acquisition costs of data for direct investment through data vendors, professional services, or self-collection can be much higher than REIT data.

Here are some advantages of owning REITs.

- *Low minimum investment.* The first, most notable difference compared to direct investment is the low investment level needed for REIT investments. Many REITs are publicly listed and traded on exchanges. Therefore, REITs trade like a stock such that an investor can take positions in the listed security. This feature provides two advantages: (1) investors don't need much money to gain exposure to the real estate market and (2) REIT investments are much more liquid than buying an income-generating property. Also, investors don't need to worry about management, maintenance, and other factors related to the properties.

- *Tax incentives.* REITs offer tax incentives to investors as income generated is typically not taxed at the corporate level. Recall, REITs pass most of the income generated from their portfolios to investors. REITs generally must distribute 90% of profits as dividends. Further, they do not pay taxes on this income before distributing dividends.

- *Availability of more complex strategies and instruments.* REITs have another advantage since the investors who manage them have access to more complex strategies and instruments. Consequently, better risk management should occur in the portfolio. If investors want to take a position against the real estate market, they can easily short the REIT's shares.

Despite these advantages, REITs have several drawbacks.

- *Fees.* One caveat to investing in REITs is the fees. If you have substantial capital, you may want to consider managing a portfolio of properties to achieve higher returns and possible economies of scale. You should compare these fees relative to potential brokerage or agent fees paid during a direct property transaction, reducing profits.

- *Lack of control.* REIT investors must accept the decisions of the management team. Thus, a poorly managed REIT may suffer losses. You may opt to take on direct property management if you feel able to do so.

3.12. WHAT IS REAL ESTATE CROWDFUNDING?

Crowdfunding is a modern development in capital raising that uses social media to attract small to mid-sized investors to pool funds for an idea, company, product, or similar venture. At one time, the SEC only allowed accredited investors to participate in crowdfunding campaigns, but it has now lifted those bans. Consequently, investors with small capital pools can join in the capital-raising process. The Jumpstart Our Business Start-ups (JOBS) Act of 2012 made crowdfunding possible, with the SEC lifting the ban on non-accredited investors in 2015. The Act's purpose was to lift barriers for small businesses to raise capital. Typically, crowdfunding campaigns are directed toward equity transactions, granting investors small equity stakes in the company raising funds. However, real estate transactions now increasingly receive crowdfunding with investment minimums as low as $5,000. Similar to equity crowdfunding, real estate transactions grant investors a stake in the property. Some of a property's profits are "passed through" to investors rather than receiving an

> *"Landlords grow rich in their sleep without working, risking or economising."*
>
> John Stuart Mill

ownership stake in a company. Crowdfunding can serve as a means for investors with smaller capital pools or who don't want to invest in REITs to gain exposure to real estate diversification benefits at generally low costs.

Limitations placed by the SEC on non-accredited investors reduce the risk of crowdfunding efforts.

- If either net worth or annual income is less than $107,000 annually, an investor can only invest the greater of either $2,200 or 5% of annual income or net worth, whichever is less.

- If net worth and annual income are at least $107,000 annually, an investor can invest up to 10% of net worth or annual income, whichever is less, but not exceed $107,000.

3.13. WHAT METHODS ARE AVAILABLE FOR MEASURING THE RETURN OF A REAL ESTATE INVESTMENT?

Several methods are available for calculating returns on real estate. This task isn't easy because of the multi-period nature of real estate investments. Additionally, many vital variables are time-varying, like vacancy rates and cap rates. Below is a more detailed discussion of different methods: (1) internal rate of return (IRR), (2) return on equity (ROE), (3) cash-on-cash, (4) equity multiple, and (5) income yield plus appreciation yield.

- *IRR.* The *IRR* of an investment is the discount rate that brings the net present value of all potential cash flows to zero. It allows a suitable "apples-to-apples" comparison of different potential investments and is a good check as to whether an investor should accept a project. One caveat is that the IRR method doesn't incorporate external factors that may affect cash flows, such as potential inflation and changes in the cost of capital. Equation (3.3) shows the formula to calculate IRR:

$$0 = \text{NPV} = \sum_{t=1}^{T} \frac{\text{CF}_t}{\left(1 + \text{IRR}\right)^t} - \text{CF}_0, \qquad (3.3)$$

where CF_t is the net cash flow during period t, CF_0 is the total investment cost or the net cash flow at period 0, and T is the number of periods.

- *ROE. ROE* is a measure of how effectively an asset generates profits. Investors should compare ROE to a peer benchmark to determine whether it's at an acceptable level. As Equation (3.4) shows, ROE's calculation involves dividing net income by shareholders' equity. Specifically, for real estate, you must use an investor's equity in a property

$$\text{ROE} = \frac{\text{Net Income}}{\text{Shareholders' Equity}}. \qquad (3.4)$$

Inventors can use ROE metrics as a baseline to build growth estimates of a property or potential investment and determine whether a particular investment is worth accepting over another.

- *Cash-on-cash. The cash-on-cash rate of return* expresses the income generated on the cash that someone has invested in a property. For example, for cash-on-cash measures, shown in Equation (3.5), the return made on a property relative to the mortgage paid on the property during the same period is

$$\text{Cash} - \text{on} - \text{Cash} = \frac{\text{Annual Pre} - \text{Tax Cash Flow}}{\text{Total Invested}}, \qquad (3.5)$$

where Equation (3.6) determines the annual pre-tax cash flow:

$$\text{APTCF} = \big(\text{Gross Scheduled Rent} + \text{Other Income}\big)$$
$$- (\text{Vacancy} + \text{Operating Expense} \qquad (3.6)$$
$$+ \text{Annual Mortgage Payments}).$$

Since cash-on-cash or cash yield metrics include mortgage payments, they're essential measures to understand and determine when comparing lending terms and feasibility.

• *Equity multiple.* An equity multiple is one of the most common and important metrics used in evaluating real estate performance. Investors use equity multiples to compare the return/cash flows generated over an investment's life to the investment's total cost. Thus, equity multiples are similar to the cash-on-cash method but are calculated over the investment's life or a multi-year period and measure the cash generated per $1 invested. In contrast, cash-on-cash is as a percent-yield over a single year period, as Equation (3.7) shows,

$$\text{Equity Multiple} = \frac{\text{Total Cash Flows}}{\text{Total Invested}}. \qquad (3.7)$$

For instance, if an individual bought a property for $2 million, generated $500,000 in cash flows annually over six years, and then sold the property for $3 million, the equity multiple is 3, meaning for every $1 invested, the investor earned $3 at the end of the investment's life (pre-tax).

• *Income yield + Appreciation yield.* Generally, yield measures the return on an investment's total cost against its annual income (income yield). Income yield, shown in Equation

(3.8), is similar to a property's cap rate. However, instead of accounting for the property's price/value, it uses the investment's total cost, which can serve as a more accurate empirical measure of performance

$$\text{Income Yield } (\%) = \frac{\text{Annual Income}}{\text{Total Cost}}. \qquad (3.8)$$

Investors can measure income yield as levered or unlevered yield. The unlevered yield metric assumes that the investor only uses equity or cash to invest or finance the property investment. Levered yield measures the yield when an investor uses some form of debt to finance the property investment. Generally, a levered yield is larger than an unlevered yield, because the total investment cost tends to be lower due to the lesser amount of capital (equity) needed to invest in the property. The investor takes out a mortgage and only has to provide a down payment plus pay the loan's cost, which affects the annual income generated.

For example, a property investor pays $2 million to buy a rental-home and spends $1 million renovating. The investor expects to generate an NOI of $300,000 annually, bringing the unlevered yield to 10%. However, what happens if the investor takes out a mortgage to finance this transaction? The investor takes out a $2 million loan to finance the transaction and only has to put up $1 million of the investor's capital. However, due to financing costs, the expected NOI is lowered to only $200,000. The levered yield increases to 20%.

> "Real estate cannot be lost or stolen, nor can it be carried away. Purchased with common sense, paid for in full, and managed with reasonable care, it is about the safest investment in the world."
> Franklin D. Roosevelt

Appreciation yield doesn't consider cash flows or potential income and only accounts for the property's rise in value over time. For instance, if an investor buys a $2 million property and its value appreciates to $2.5 million over five years, the appreciation yield would be 25%.

Using both appreciation yield and income yield allows investors to account for and measure multiple factors that may affect their investment's total performance over its lifespan and enables a better comparison between different properties and investment decisions.

3.14. HOW DOES REAL ESTATE COMPARE TO OTHER ASSET CLASSES IN A PORTFOLIO ALLOCATION STRATEGY?

Real estate as an investment class provides several advantages for inclusion in a traditional portfolio. Some of these benefits are listed below:

- *Diversification.* Real estate provides diversification benefits when optimally allocated into a portfolio. Historically, real estate is an asset that exhibits a relatively low correlation to equity markets, which provides a strong hedge against potential volatility. However, different sectors and economic conditions affect these correlations, and investors should frequently reevaluate their allocation strategies as conditions change.

  > *"Now, one thing I tell everyone is learn about real estate. Repeat after me: real estate provides the highest returns, the greatest values and the least risk."*
  >
  > Armstrong Williams

- *Alternative to fixed-income allocations.* Real estate is an attractive alternative to fixed-income allocations. It provides a relatively stable income over long investment horizons while also retaining potential capital appreciation. A bond's principal or par value doesn't generally change over its lifespan.

- *Inflation hedge.* Real estate also serves as a strong hedge against inflation. During inflationary periods, the value of properties and rent levels typically rise, providing positive upside exposure to the inflationary environment. Of course, this relation may not always hold during every inflationary period. Thus, investors should be aware of how much of their portfolio is allocated to inflation protection, and real estate as an overallocation could result in large risks.

> "Don't wait to buy real estate, buy real estate and wait."
> T. Harv Eker

Overall, real estate has its benefits as a diversification and hedging tool to investors' managing portfolios. Whether allocators are looking to diversify their risk exposures, hedge inflation, or even diversify their cash flow profiles, investors need to understand what potential new exposures they're introducing to a portfolio when allocating to real estate. For instance, while real estate usually exhibits a low correlation to other asset classes, some sectors like industrial, commercial real estate may show a high correlation with some manufacturing sectors or companies. Thus, savvy investors avoid allocating heavily to properties in that same sector if they're already heavily invested in industrial production firms.

3.15. WHAT IS A MORTGAGE, AND HOW ARE MORTGAGE RATES DETERMINED?

As mentioned previously, a *mortgage* is a loan backed (collateralized) by the property itself. The borrower is obligated to make the contractual mortgage payments or risk default. Most mortgages have a fixed rate for their entire term (usually 15 or 30 years), but some are adjustable, called *adjustable-rate mortgages* (ARMs). In a fixed-rate mortgage, the bank is at risk if the homeowner decides to refinance at lower rates. *Refinancing* is when the borrower replaces a high interest loan with a lower interest rate loan. In an ARM, the borrower bears the risk of higher future interest rates.

Both borrower and economy-wide factors determine mortgage rates. Character, income, and credit history are essential factors determining the interest rate from a personal standpoint. A FICO score (i.e., credit score) summarizes an individual's credit history. FICO is an acronym for the Fair Isaac Corporation, which is the company that pioneered the credit score calculation. Similarly, the level of inflation and other macro factors affect the rates at which banks are willing to lend. Another factor influencing mortgage rates is a loan's duration: longer loans typically have higher interest rates. However, many 30-year mortgages don't last 30 years because homeowners may move, refinance, or get divorced. Thus, the effective life is much closer to 10 years. Therefore, a close tie exists between 30-year mortgage rates and movements in the 10-year Treasury bond yield.

3.16. WHAT KIND OF LENDERS ARE AVAILABLE, AND HOW DO THEY DIFFER?

Most real estate investors, especially novices, borrow via a traditional mortgage. However, the interest rate is likely to be higher for investment property than that of owner-occupied real estate. The lender's terms are more stringent than for a primary residence. Some borrowers can put less than 20% down payment if they qualify for government programs such as for veterans. The lower the down payment, the higher is the leverage and potential profit. Another alternative is to borrow against the equity in another property through a home equity line of credit (HELOC). A HELOC is essentially a credit card against the equity in a real estate investment. This method is a quick and easy way to secure funds.

Commercial real estate loans typically have shorter terms and higher rates compared to residential mortgages. These loans may also have prepayment penalties. Additionally, commercial real estate loans are useful for investors wanting to buy and flip a home since the terms are more flexible than traditional primary residence purchases. Investors and non-traditional banks fund some commercial loans. These loans are known as *hard money loans* that can result in funding in days instead of months for traditional mortgages.

A new phenomenon has also emerged via peer-to-peer (P2P) lending. P2P platforms connect borrowers with lenders. Since these relationships are literally between strangers, the P2P platform earns fees, and the offered rate is typically higher than a traditional mortgage.

3.17. WHAT FACTORS DO MORTGAGE LENDERS EXAMINE?

Mortgage lenders are primarily concerned with receiving the monthly payments the borrower has promised. Part of the due diligence process is to verify the borrower's income and other liabilities. Higher income and lower liabilities increase

> *"Find out where the people are going and buy the land before they get there."*
> William Penn Adair

the size of the mortgage and may decrease the interest rate. Lenders also require a down payment, which is generally 20% of the purchase price. This payment is a buffer. If the property value decreases, the bank can still recover its funds. Over time, the loan balance goes down, and hopefully, the property value goes up. This ratio is called the *loan-to-value* (LTV) ratio. So, a 20% down payment is equivalent to an 80% LTV. Lenders will also verify the source of the down payment to make sure that the applicant didn't borrow it.

> "It is a comfortable feeling to know that you stand on your own ground. Land is about the only thing that can't fly away."
> Anthony Trollope

3.18. WHAT HAPPENS IN A FORECLOSURE?

A *foreclosure* occurs when the borrower can't pay the mortgage. Homeowners want to pay their mortgage and keep their home, but sometimes circumstances such as job loss or health concerns make paying a mortgage difficult. After 30 days, the lender considers the loan delinquent and, after 90 days, seriously delinquent. Homeowners who fall behind payments find catching up increasingly difficult. The bank may try to restructure the loan, sometimes called "pretend and extend." The bank may also arrange a *short sale* – a real estate sale in which the net proceeds from selling the property fall short of the debts secured by liens against the property. The lender may place the property up for auction. This situation could provide an opportunity for investors. If the property doesn't sell, it becomes part of the bank's real estate-owned portfolio.

3.19. WHAT TAX ADVANTAGES AND DISADVANTAGES ARE SPECIFIC TO REAL ESTATE?

The main tax benefit for homeowners is the tax-deductibility of interest. The amount of interest paid to the bank reduces the taxable income for the borrower. This tax break is a rare opportunity where the government is subsidizing your purchase! Consider a $100,000 mortgage with 4% annual interest rate. The borrower pays $4,000 interest in the first year (4% of $100,000). However, the homeowner reduces their taxable income by $4,000, effectively saving income tax on $4,000. If the borrower has a marginal tax rate of 30%, the borrower's income taxes decrease by $1,200 (30% of $4,000 interest). Hence, the net cost of the interest is only $2,800, or a 2.8% effective rate.

An investment property also allows the deductibility of interest but offers a depreciation benefit, since the property's depreciation in the current period reduces the income from the investment. So, the tax bill each period is lower than otherwise. You might ask why the government allows this treatment. After the property's sale, taxes are due on the difference between the selling price and depreciated basis. This depreciation recapture increases the tax bill at the time of the sale. But recall that delaying taxes is a good strategy, and the long-term capital gains tax rate is likely lower than the current period income tax rate. This situation greatly benefits the borrower, and it gets better. Some attractive provisions for investors are also available to exchange the property with no immediate tax liability. These deals, called 1031 exchanges, occur when selling a property but repurchasing a similar ("like-kind") type. This process effectively delays capital gains indefinitely.

3.20. WHAT COMMON MISTAKES DO INVESTORS MAKE IN REAL ESTATE?

Although real estate investing has excellent potential, investors should avoid some common mistakes.

- *Insufficient planning.* As simple as it sounds, planning and understanding is the first step to any investment decision. Understanding your investment goals is also essential. Is the investment commercial or residential property? How long do you plan on holding this property? How much capital do you have available? What's your risk tolerance? Will you be flipping this property, renting it, or taking some other action? How will you finance the property? Planning is critical because it helps you set forth expectations and understand how you expect to enter and exit the investment.

> *"There are three things that matter in property: location, location, location."*
> Unknown author

- *Lack of due diligence.* Once you have identified a plan of action, another critical step involves research. The due diligence that accompanies a real estate transaction must be rigorous and extensive, as with any investment decision. Being informed about the property, like its location, tax implications, and potential tenants, is critical.

- *Inappropriate financing structure.* Arguably, financing is as important as the planning and due diligence phases because poor financing structures can ruin a property's return potential. For instance, an ARM may result in you paying a much higher rate if interest rates rise, increasing the financing cost, which reduces a property's rate of return.

- *Unawareness of all costs.* You need to be aware of all costs associated with the initial investment, such as a down payment on a mortgage, closing costs, legal fees, agent fees, and bank fees. Many savvy investors tend to budget for initial costs to include all of those costs plus at least three months of runway (excess capital) to allow for operation or even renovation until they find tenants or in the event of any unforeseen expenses.

- *Failure to maintain a professional network.* First-time real estate investors may believe they can conduct the entire transaction on their own. Well, it's not that easy. You must develop and maintain relationships with local bankers, lawyers, real estate agents, management companies, maintenance, and others to create a strong network that can benefit you in the event of a market downturn. Further, a robust professional network may allow for more advantageous financing options, better pricing for services, and increased leads to additional properties/tenants.

- *Lack of awareness of the local market.* Although systemic risks can adversely affect real estate, the local market is the basis of much of real estate's risk profile. Each area or neighborhood has varying building codes, tenant demographics, tax regimes, and a host of other factors. Therefore, you need to understand the local market to maximize your return and minimize potential risk exposures. You also need to understand what tenants are attracted to a property. Neglecting tenants' needs can severely affect a real estate investment's performance, as ultimately, they're the ones paying the rent that generates cash flow.

3.21. WHAT ARE SOME ONLINE RESOURCES FOR REAL ESTATE?

Various online resources are available for real estate investing.

> *"Buy real estate in areas where the path exists…and buy more real estate where there is no path, but you can create your own."*
> David Waronker

- Millionacres (https://www.fool.com/millionacres/), a Motley Fool company, provides useful information on how to invest in real estate.

- National Association of REITs (https://www.reit.com/) offers a wealth of information on REITs.

- Bigger pockets (https://www.biggerpockets.com/) helps smaller investors with real estate investing.

- Adventuresincre.com (https://www.adventuresincre.com/) has information on commercial real estate modeling and careers.

- The Urban Land Institute (https://uli.org/) provides resources and discussion on real estate and land usage.

- NAIOP.org discusses critical issues related to commercial real estate.

- CoStar (https://www.costar.com/) is a leading commercial real estate data provider but requires a subscription.

- Real Estate Solutions by Moody's Analytics (https://www.reis.com/) provides valuable commercial real estate information but requires a subscription.

- GetREFM.com offers real estate modeling resources and certification.

TAKEAWAYS

Real estate investing can take many forms from equity to debt, public to private, and hands-on to hands-off. Real estate is an integral part of a diversified portfolio. Thus, savvy investors should be aware of this chapter's key takeaways.

- Get to know the real estate market and its unique characteristics.

- Do your homework before investing in any type of real estate.

- Choose the appropriate real estate style to fit your needs: core, core-plus, value-add, and opportunistic investments.

- Treat direct real estate investments as a business with purposeful planning, execution, and management.

- Have multiple exit strategies if you invest directly in real estate.

- Be aware that rental properties aren't necessarily suitable investments.

- Diversify your portfolio by adding real estate, especially using low-cost real estate mutual funds and ETFs.

- Use REITs as the easiest way to gain exposure to real estate.

- Understand the challenges of measuring the return of residential real estate.

- Know the tax laws involving real estate.

4

INVESTING IN COMMODITIES: GETTING AN INFLATION HEDGE

"Commodities such as gold and silver have a world market that transcends national borders, politics, religions, and race. A person may not like someone else's religion, but he'll accept his gold."

Robert Kiyosaki, American Businessman
and Author

Commodities have a long and storied history. Early markets can be traced back around 6,000 years to Sumeria (livestock) and China (rice). Countless tales are available of kings, emperors, and pirates searching and hoarding gold and jewels to build their wealth. In particular, gold and other precious metals seem to capture our imagination as a way to measure wealth regardless of geographic boundaries or period. Generally, commodities are physical products or essential inputs to the products you consume and rely upon each day. These items include the grain in your bread and cereal, the crude oil in your gasoline, and the copper wiring in your house. Commodities are considered *real assets*, which are tangible assets with a physical substance and may be renewable

"In ancient times, we were users; we used the commodities in accordance to our needs. Using is not sufficient for the modern market; it needs consumers. Consuming means consuming things much more than the natural need of humanity or any living being."

Lobsang Tenzin

(wheat and lumber) or non-renewable (natural gas or gold). Because of their physical nature, commodities must be stored and transported to the end-user or intermediary. The commodity needs to be refined for commercial use (crude oil) or used as an input for other consumption purposes (soybeans). Although you may be aware of the wide range of commodities, you may be unfamiliar with the investment opportunities related to them. Rest assured, modern financial markets provide many pathways for you to participate in individual or pooled commodity investments.

Intuitively, supply and demand serve as the basis of commodity values: the greater the demand, the higher the price. Similarly, the smaller the supply, the higher the price. The end-user, such as a miller who needs the grain to make flour to sell to customers, determines the demand for commodities. Simultaneously, the farmer plants the seeds, tills the fields, and waits to bring the wheat harvest to market. In the meantime, a drought, flood, changing demand, and many other factors may affect wheat's future selling prices. Such events introduce the hedger and speculator as critical players in a market. A *hedger*, who could be either the producer or the end-user, is a market participant who wants to avoid future price uncertainty. In contrast, a *speculator* is someone willing to bear the future price uncertainty. Consider a farmer who is uncertain about the future price of wheat. As a result, the farmer accepts a relatively lower price to guarantee the wheat's sale at harvest time. In this scenario, the farmer shifts the price risk to the buyer, who is the end-user. *Price risk* is the risk that the value of a security or an investment will decrease. To induce the end-user to bear the price risk, the seller must offer a lower price. In

> *"When you look at a commodities market you need hedgers and speculators. If you don't have one, you don't have a market. That's how it works."*
> T. Boone Pickens

this case, the farmer is the hedger and the buyer is the speculator. Of course, wheat is such a critical input to the end-user that the end-user may be willing to lock in a relatively high price today to guarantee access to the raw material. In this case, the end-user is the hedger. This simplified example illustrates the interplay between hedgers and speculators in determining the *price for future delivery*, also called the *commodity's futures price*.

An individual would seemingly be unlikely to buy a commodity, store it, and sell it later for a higher price. This strategy of "buy and hold" isn't practical for most commodities, particularly for small investors. You can more easily "buy and hold" financial assets such as stocks and bonds and even the hedge fund and private equity (PE) investments discussed in this book. How then can you participate and profit in the commodities market? If you don't want to buy the

> *"Stock prices can go to zero. Commodities cannot. Unlike shares in a company commodities are real things that are always likely to be worth something to somebody."*
> Jim Rogers

actual good, you can enter commodity markets by investing in
(1) shares of individual companies that search, extract, refine,
and produce commodities; (2) mutual funds or exchange-
traded fund (ETF) shares of such companies; (3) mutual
funds or ETFs based on a basket or portfolio of commodities;
or (4) futures contracts. Let's now turn our attention to the
exciting world of commodity investing.

4.1. WHAT ARE COMMODITIES AND THEIR PRIMARY ATTRIBUTES?

Commodities are consumption assets that at some point are
actually used and then cease to exist. They are building blocks
of the global economy. The physical commodity isn't typically an investment. However, precious metals like gold are
an exception because they
aren't used up and can be
resold later in the same condition. Instead, commodities
are the physical raw materials directly consumed or part
of the production process
for other consumed prod-
ucts. For example, people consume orange juice directly but
need to refine crude oil before it becomes gasoline or diesel
for your vehicle. Commodities are less liquid than financial
assets because of the storage, transportation, and insurance
costs associated with ownership but are more liquid than
real estate. Established markets are available for many commodities and commodity derivatives. A *derivative* is a financial security whose value depends on or is derived from some
observable price or process such as interest rates, commodity
prices, or index levels.

> *"Formula for success:
> rise early, work hard,
> strike oil."*
>   J. Paul Getty

Because of their physical nature, an asset's quality may differ from sample to sample and between locations. For example, consider two different crude oil grades: West Texas Intermediate (WTI) and Brent. It's not surprising that WTI, extracted from the southern United States and the Gulf of Mexico, has slightly different chemical properties than Brent, originating in the North Atlantic region. These distinctions are sufficiently

> *"Gold and silver, like other commodities, have an intrinsic value, which is not arbitrary, but is dependent on their scarcity, the quantity of labour bestowed in procuring them, and the value of the capital employed in the mines which produce them."*
> David Ricardo

meaningful to result in substantial pricing differences based on the amount of refining needed to bring each grade to its useable form for the end-user.

4.2. WHAT ARE THE MOST COMMON TYPES OF COMMODITIES?

Several ways are available to divide and describe the commodity space. Some classify commodities as hard or soft. *Hard commodities* are mined or extracted from the earth, such as gold, oil, copper, or natural gas. Countries endowed with sizeable natural resource commodities provide a significant source of wealth. For example, Australia, Canada, Saudi Arabia, and South Africa have large reserves of hard commodities. In contrast, *soft commodities* require effort to bring the product to market, including farming and physical care. Some examples of soft commodities include cocoa, soybeans, and livestock. Although hard commodities tend to be fungible or interchangeable, soft commodities may vary more in quality based on geography and environmental factors. For example, Columbia's cocoa beans result from the local ecological factors of humidity, soil, and temperature.

Another way to classify commodities is by sector such as energy, metals, and agricultural. A brief discussion of each sector follows.

> "We will not allow our country ever to be at the mercy of commodity price volatility or external markets."
>
> Mohammad bin Salman

- *Energy*. Energy commodities include crude oil, natural gas, and coal. As mentioned previously, several grades of crude oil are available, including WTI (the United States and the Gulf of Mexico), Brent (North Atlantic), and Bonny (Nigeria). The classification of each grade depends on its sweetness (low amount of sulfur) or sourness (high amount of sulfur). In general, crude oil with less sulfur requires less refining and demands a higher price. Around 100 grades of crude oil are available, but WTI, Brent, and OPEC, which is oil from the 13 Organization of the Petroleum Exporting Countries, are the most economically important. Crude oil helps to power transportation (e.g., cars, planes, and ships) and serves as a component used in plastics, cosmetics, fertilizer, and many other products.

  Consumers use natural gas primarily for heating and cooling their homes and businesses. Natural gas also powers turbines to generate electricity. Advances in logistics allow liquified natural gas to be shipped worldwide, deepening the available global supply. Natural gas is a relatively clean energy source with less impact on global warming than oil and coal. Russia, Iran, Qatar, and the United States have large natural gas reserves.

> *"Prudence is what makes someone a great commodities trader - the capacity to face reality squarely in the eye without allowing emotion or ego to get in the way. It's what is needed by every quarterback or battlefield general."*
> John Ortberg

Coal is a cheap but dirtier energy source than natural gas. Nonetheless, it still provides about 50% of the electrical needs worldwide. The United States, Russia, and China have large natural deposits of coal. For developing and emerging economies like China, reliance on cheap energy such as coal is essential.

- *Metals*. The name is self-explanatory. You've undoubtedly heard of the most common metals, those known as *precious metals*. Precious metals include gold, silver, platinum, and palladium. The scarcity of these metals may provide inflation protection as investors search for "flight to quality" during economic stress. *Flight-to-quality*, also called *flight-to-safety*, is a financial market phenomenon

> *"Since the start of the new millennium, more investors have begun to move into commodity investments."*
> David Rodeck

occurring when investors sell what they perceive to be higher-risk investments and buy safer assets, such as gold and other precious metals. Thus, gold traditionally acts as a haven when traditional markets fall.

The base metals include iron, copper, zinc, nickel, aluminum, tin, and lead. Because base metals are much more abundant than precious metals, their prices are much lower. Base metals prices relate directly to the demand for their end products like steel beams used in construction. The 17 rare-earth metals, such as cerium, yttrium, lanthanum, and neodymium, aren't rare but are found in many locations globally and hard to extract. Uses of these metals include electronics such as cell phones and military applications. In general, metals aren't highly seasonal and have lower storage costs than agricultural products.

> "The truth in acting is that we are all hired help. We are a commodity. There is no difference between being an actor and pork bellies."
> Lorraine Bracco

- *Agricultural.* Agricultural commodities include products used for food consumption (e.g., rice, wheat, and soybeans) and industrial and manufacturing needs (e.g., lumber and wool). The primary categories are cereal grains, oilseeds, meat, dairy, and others. Cereal grains, including wheat, corn, oats, barley, and rough rice, often serve as feed for livestock and human consumption. Oilseeds include canola, cotton, palm oil, and soybeans. The livestock (meat) category comprises feeder cattle, live cattle, lean hogs, and pork bellies. Dairy products consist of milk, butter, whey, and cheese. Examples of other commodities are cocoa, coffee, sugar, and frozen concentrated orange juice. Organized markets are also available for lumber, rubber, and wool.

4.3. WHAT ARE THE ADVANTAGES OF INVESTING IN COMMODITIES?

Commodities offer several benefits for investors, including inflation hedging, added diversification, high-potential returns, and a convenience yield.

- *Potential hedge against inflation.* Many view commodities as inflation hedges since commodity prices generally rise with inflation. Because commodities are necessary inputs, inflation tends to increase the price of both commodities and the end product.

- *Diversification.* Investors can also use commodities as diversifiers in a portfolio as their historical correlation with equities is less than one. *Correlation* is a statistical measure that captures the degree to which two variables or factors move together. A correlation of one indicates that the two factors move in lockstep with each other, and so provide no diversification benefit. Commodities exhibit a negative correlation with equities during some periods, meaning that as the returns for one asset class increase, the other tends to decrease, and vice versa. Having negatively correlated investments in a portfolio is beneficial, because it reduces a portfolio's overall volatility and hence risk. Over time, both commodities and commodity stocks generally provide returns that differ from stocks and bonds. However, diversification doesn't ensure a profit or guarantee against a loss.

- *High-potential returns.* Investing in commodities offers the potential for high returns. For example, demand for various commodities increases due to massive global infrastructure projects may lead to a rise in commodity prices, positively affecting stock prices in related industries and resulting in higher returns.

- *Convenience yield.* A third advantage of investing in commodities involves a *convenience yield*, a non-monetary benefit that accrues to the asset holder. Oil is an example of a product with a potentially high convenience yield. If you own the physical oil directly, you can manage its production and reap the rewards from its shortage when selling it for higher prices. Although the convenience yield is hard to quantify, having access to critical raw material input, such as wheat for a cereal manufacturer, could be an important benefit. However, you can only imply the convenience yield value because you still face risk in carrying the position.

- *Lease rate.* Another potential benefit of owning commodities is the asset owner's ability to lease the asset to another market participant. For example, the commodity owner can temporarily lend or transfer the physical commodity for a fee. Gold is the most common commodity to be leased to another party. The monetary return earned is called the *lease rate.*

4.4. WHAT ARE THE POTENTIAL DISADVANTAGES OF INVESTING IN COMMODITIES?

Despite their attractive features, commodities have some drawbacks.

- *No income generation.* Commodities don't generate any cash flow. They provide no dividends or interest as with stocks and bonds. An investor only receives the price at the point of sale, which may be in the distant future.

- *High volatility.* Commodity prices may experience considerable fluctuations due to such factors as world events, economic conditions, import controls, worldwide competition, and government regulations. Thus, by investing in commodities, you face *principal risk*, which is the chance that your investment could lose money. As Table 4.1 shows, commodity prices may have extremely high volatility. The variation in returns within the same year is striking. For example, during 2010, palladium experienced a 96.6% gain, but natural gas suffered a 30.7% loss. A massive difference also exists for silver returns between the two periods, specifically, 2010 (83.2%) and 2020 (3.4%). As a rough estimate, commodities are about twice as

Table 4.1. Historical Commodity Returns

Commodity	Performance (2010) %	Performance (2015) %	Performance (2020) %
Palladium	96.6	−34.0	−2.7
Crude oil	19.4	−36.4	−20.5
Nickel	33.9	−42.1	26.1
Platinum	20.8	−25.9	−0.1
Gold	29.5	−10.7	2.3
Silver	83.2	−14.3	3.4
Wheat	46.7	−12.7	22.4
Corn	51.7	−5.2	25.1
Copper	31.4	−25.7	30.3
Aluminum	12.0	−17.9	11.6
Lead	6.7	−2.8	7.1
Zinc	−3.4	−27.8	−0.9
Coal	31.4	−10.7	52.1
Natural gas	−30.7	−23.6	21.1

Source: Bloomberg.

Note: This table shows the annual return for various commodities in 2010, 2015, and 2020.

volatile as stocks and four times as volatile as bonds. Thus, given the large swings in prices, commodity companies can experience substantial gains or losses.

"Growth without diversification, technological improvement, and increased productivity is easily reversed: all it takes is a dip in commodity prices."
Arancha Gonzalez

- *Additional costs*. Investors in a physical commodity must anticipate and price the storage, transportation, and insurance costs. The commodity holder absorbs these costs, much like a landlord who must expend resources to maintain a property.

- *Potential market manipulation*. The whims of a small group of traders or investors who want to keep prices at a certain level can manipulate some markets such as crude oil and diamonds.

- *Closely related to global economic growth*. If the global economy slows down, so does the demand for many commodities, thus reducing the expected diversification benefits.

4.5. HOW CAN INVESTORS TRADE COMMODITIES?

Commodities, like all investments, have their own set of risks and rewards. Once you decide that you want to invest in commodities, you must decide on how to invest. Commodity markets have both *spot* and *futures* markets. A *spot market* denotes the price for immediate payment and delivery/

acceptance of the commodity. Individuals rarely engage in spot market transactions, because they don't have the physical means to transport and store the commodity. Also, they typically don't consume the item. Instead, the overwhelming majority of trading activity occurs in the futures markets. A *futures contract* specifies the future date for delivery and other factors such as location, grade, and amount. Futures contracts for commodities historically traded on organized exchanges such as the Chicago Board of Trade, Chicago Mercantile Exchange (CME), or New York Mercantile Exchange. Despite the much greater volume in futures markets, investors close out almost all contracts before maturity. Traders close out their contracts, because they rarely want to take actual delivery or physically own the asset to deliver. For example, if an investor is long a July expiry WTI futures, the investor sells a July expiry WTI futures to close the position and receives (pay) any profit (loss).

> *"Deep down I knew if Hell existed, it was a real place of ruthless, venal people, like the commodity pits at the Chicago Board of Trade, Disney World, or oral arguments before the United States Supreme Court."*
> Richard Dooling

As an individual investor, you may qualify for a futures account with your brokerage firm. Although the contract size might be relatively large, you benefit from the market's deep liquidity and transparency. Plus, the posting of margin (collateral) and the central clearinghouse structure remove almost all the counterparty (performance) risk. *Counterparty risk* is the risk that the counterparty in the trade doesn't transact. In short, each side of a transaction posts margin held by the futures exchange, which serves as the central

136 The Savvy Investor's Guide to Building Wealth

counterparty (CCP) to all traders. The CCP moves the gains and losses daily to and from one account to another, called *mark-to-market*. If the collateral account gets too low, the CCP demands cash or securities or closes out the investor's position. Therefore, the CCP doesn't absorb a loss as the proverbial middleman.

4.6. HOW CAN RETAIL INVESTORS GET STARTED IN INVESTING IN COMMODITIES?

Investing in commodities is as easy as investing in stocks and bonds. Although many choices are available, some are better suited for individual investors than others.

- *Buy physical commodities.* Novice investors should probably steer away from directly buying physical commodities. As previously discussed, storage and transportation costs are impractical for most. Although you probably don't want to store hundreds of oil drums in your home, you might want to hold gold bullion or gold coins. Gold has an active secondary market, and a price point of around $1,795 per troy ounce (December 2020) is low enough that retail investors could buy and hold the physical asset. An alternative is to simply buy a gold ETF that closely tracks the price changes in the gold market. The SPDR Gold ETF (GLD)

> "Prudence is what makes someone a great commodities trader – the capacity to face reality squarely in the eye without allowing emotion or ego to get in the way. It's what is needed by every quarterback or battlefield general."
> John Ortberg

is one of the most actively traded ETFs and closely tracks the gold bullion price. The SPDR Gold MiniShares (GLDM) also tracks gold bullion at a fraction (1/10) of the cost of GLD.

- *Invest in shares of commodity producers.* Another way to access the commodity market is by investing in the shares of commodity producers such as mineral and mining firms and oil exploration firms. Freeport-McMoRan (FCX) and ExxonMobil (XOM) are two examples, respectively. A close tie exists between these firms' value and the overall movement in the underlying commodity price. Of course, firm-specific factors such as accounting fraud, higher than expected extraction costs, or political uncertainty in foreign countries are likely to reduce investor returns. Similarly, you can buy shares of agricultural companies that grow or resell crops to food producers. Tyson Foods (TSN) and Archer-Daniels-Midland (ADM) provide exposure to livestock and grains, respectively.

> *"The exchangeable value of all commodities, rises as the difficulties of their production increase."*
> David Ricardo

- *Buy commodity mutual funds and ETFs.* An easy alternative for investors to gain exposure to commodity markets is through mutual funds and ETFs. Both types of pooled investment vehicles (PIVs) invest in a diversified pool of commodities or commodity-producing companies. The low minimum investment size and high liquidity of PIVs are attractive features. Many choices are available, ranging from broadly diversified investments to narrower choices. Of course, more predictability and less risk exist with diversified PIVs compared to more focused

PIVs. Some popular examples of commodity ETFs are SPDR Gold Trust (GLD), PowerShares DB Commodity Index Tracking (DBC), and United States Oil Fund (USO). The GLD ETF provides returns based on gold's performance, whereas DBC tracks an index based on multiple commodities. The VanEck Gold Miners (GDX) doesn't invest in the commodity directly but rather in companies actively mining for gold. Thus, you have ample opportunities to choose broad or narrow commodity exposure.

- *Investing in futures.* Investing with futures contracts is a bit more advanced but easily accessible to individual investors. Futures contracts are simply commitments to buy (long) or sell (short) a fixed amount of a commodity at a set price on a set date. The Security Exchange Commission and Commodity Futures Trading Commission (CFTC) regulate futures markets. Although most contract terms are standardized, some contracts have flexibility in the timing and location of delivery. Therefore, buyers of futures contracts are bullish, betting on rising commodity prices, while sellers of futures contracts anticipate falling commodity prices. One limitation can be a contract's size, which the exchange offering the contract sets. For example, the basis of a gold futures contract is 100 ounces of gold. Thus, if gold is $1,800 an ounce, the value of the contract is $180,000. Although the investor posts margin of less than $180,000, the amount is much higher than the minimum investment in commodity ETFs. Suppose the price of gold was $2,000 at the expiration of the futures contract. The profit to the long (buyer) would be $20,000 ($200 per ounce based on 100 ounces as specified in the contract). Similarly, the short position would suffer a loss of $20,000.

Futures exchanges such as the CME set the terms of contracts, including contract size, potential delivery dates, minimum and maximum spreads, maximum daily price limits, and return methodology. For example,

> *"I don't look at myself as a commodity, but I'm sure a lot of people have."*
> Marilyn Monroe

some details for wheat contracts are as follows:

- The basis of each wheat futures contract is 5,000 bushels.

- Acceptable variations include No. 2 Soft Red Winter, No. 2 Hard Red Winter, and several other varieties.

- Wheat with 13.5% moisture is ineligible for delivery.

- Contracts expire only in five months – July, September, December, March, and May.

- The minimum price variation is ¼ cent per bushel or $12.50 per contract.

4.7. WHAT FACTORS AFFECT THE COMMODITY MARKETS?

As an investor, you should realize that commodity markets differ from financial markets in several ways. First, financial assets have virtually no storage costs, but commodity markets do. Some commodities are highly seasonal such as natural gas, which is used more in the winter months. If an unseasonably warm winter occurs, then the supply of natural gas is likely to be abundant. Interestingly, unlike many other assets, lowering the price may not affect the demand. Think about it: no matter how cheap natural gas is, you still won't turn on your heat if your house is comfortable! This situation ties back into the importance of storage costs that the asset's physical owner must absorb.

Another critical difference is that transportation in traditional financial markets is virtually costless because of electronic and even paper transfers and record-keeping. However, commodities have substantial transportation costs – think of the cost to transport liquified natural gas from Qatar to the United States or freighting soybeans from the Midwest to the Northeast or Europe.

Finally, the pricing of financial assets reflects their risk level. Commodities are different. If anything, commodity prices tend to be mean-reverting, so periods of relatively high prices are likely to be followed by periods of lower prices. When prices are high, suppliers may bring more of the commodity to the market, but consumers may search for reasonable substitutes or alternatives. These market forces drive down prices. Conversely, if the commodity price is low, then production levels are low, which leads to an eventual increase in price and concomitant increase in supply, raising prices.

4.8. WHAT WAYS ARE AVAILABLE TO MEASURE RETURNS IN COMMODITY MARKETS?

Commodity returns can be measured using spot prices, futures prices, or computing the return of commodity indices. Comparing the current spot price relative to the price in previous periods is straightforward. This return calculation is simply the buy-and-hold return. However, this analysis ignores any storage, transportation, and insurance costs and doesn't consider the potential benefits from the convenience yield or lease rate. Recall, the convenience yield is a non-monetary benefit that investors need to estimate. Investors and analysts compute commodity indices and ETFs' returns similarly by measuring the buy-and-hold return over the investment horizon.

Measuring returns using futures contracts is more complicated. One reason for the difficulty in the return calculation is that investors generally "rollover" a new contract when the current contract expires. The simultaneous closing of an old contract and opening a new contract creates a *roll return*, also called *roll yield*. Technically, *roll yield* is the difference between the return on a futures contract relative to the spot price return. Intuitively, if prices rise, the roll return is negative because the investor buys into successively higher-priced contracts. Similarly, a positive roll return occurs if futures prices trend downward. Additionally, futures contracts are leveraged investments since the investor only needs to post the margin (collateral). Thus, the true cash-on-cash return differs from the buy-and-hold computation.

Finally, investors earn interest on their posted collateral, called the *collateral yield*. The return from the futures position is likely to differ from the spot return because of the additional costs and benefits associated with the underlying asset. Therefore, investors base the futures price on the spot price adjusted for the cost to carry (*cost of carry*) the position to expiration. Direct costs such as transportation and shipping increase the futures price, because the asset holder must absorb and receive compensation for these carrying costs. Similarly, the benefits of holding

> "The price of a commodity will never go to zero. When you invest in commodities futures, you're not buying a piece of paper that says you own an intangible piece of company that can go bankrupt."
>
> Jim Rogers

the asset (convenience and lease rate) lower the futures price. That is, the asset holder is willing to accept a lower future selling price if the asset provides benefits before expiration. The *cost of carry* is the difference between the costs and benefits. Thus, the relation between the spot and futures price is as follows: Futures price = spot price + costs – benefits.

If market conditions dictate that the costs (e.g., storage) exceed the benefits (e.g., convenience), the futures price is above the spot price. This condition is called *contango*. Another way to say this is the cost of carry is positive since costs – benefits > 0. Of course, if the benefits exceed the costs, then the futures price is below the spot price and the cost of carry < 0. A negative cost of carry means that a net benefit exists in holding the asset. This situation is called *backwardation,* or simply the market is backwardated.

4.9. WHO ARE THE PROMINENT PARTICIPANTS IN THE COMMODITIES MARKETS?

Key participants in commodity markets include commodity producers, end-users, hedgers, speculators, and institutional and retail investors. Producers include farmers, miners, lumberjacks, and related professions that tend, grow, and extract the raw materials from their source. Producers are generally the hedgers in futures markets, because they seek price certainty and accept lower prices to transfer the price risk. Speculators, who are willing to absorb the price risk, are on the opposite side of the transaction. Speculators buy at lower prices or sell at higher prices as compensation for bearing price risk. Large institutional investors, global banks, hedge funds, and sophisticated retail investors are typically the speculators. Some speculators take purely directional bets on whether market prices are likely to increase or decrease and

provide additional liquidity
to the market. *Liquidity* is
the ease by which an investor can quickly buy or sell an
asset. Speculators increase
the volume of trading activity, making trading easier
and cheaper. Arbitrageurs
seek to identify and trade
on mispricing between spot
and futures markets. Arbi-

> *"The simple two-way
> relationship between
> CPI inflation and
> the commodity price
> indexes has changed
> significantly over time."*
> Fred Furlong and
> Robert Ingenito

trageurs also provide liquidity to the market.

4.10. WHAT ARE RECENT DEVELOPMENTS IN COMMODITY MARKETS?

Due to rapid technological
advancements, the tradi-
tional physical trading ven-
ues are now less important
(New York Stock Exchange)
or closing down altogether
(Pacific Stock Exchange).
In their place are electronic
marketplaces, where buyers
and sellers don't physically
interact. Although commodity markets are no different,

> *"I have an eccentric
> view on commodities
> not necessarily shared
> by my colleagues – or
> by almost anybody.
> And that is, we're
> running out of
> everything."*
> David Ricardo

some commodity contracts such as live cattle futures still
have a traditional open outcry system. An *open outcry* system is when traders meet on the exchange floor and transact
with each other and a specialist who directs the order flow,
similar to a fast-paced auction. You may have seen pictures of

traders yelling and using hand signals to communicate; that's a trading pit.

Another trend is the increased demand from emerging markets, particularly China. The need for copper, steel, crude oil, and other commodities is likely to rise with the growth of these economies. Finally, April 2020 marks the first observation of negative futures prices (e.g., WTI crude oil) due to the COVID-19 pandemic. The dramatic drop in travel and transportation created a sudden glut and oversupply of physical crude oil, resulting in fewer facilities being physically available to store the oil until demand picked up. So, the negative price meant that the oil owners paid someone else to take the oil off their hands. This situation doesn't reflect a disconnect in the market but rather a reminder of financial markets' efficiency.

> *"It is much more convenient not be a public company. As a private company you don't have to give information to the public. Secrecy is an important factor of success in the commodity business."*
> Marc Rich

4.11. WHAT ARE COMMON COMMODITY INDICES?

Many commodity indices track individual commodity products as well as baskets of different commodities. Investors use these indices to track the underlying assets' performance and act as performance benchmarks for commodity-focused investment firms. One of the most followed indices is the S&P Goldman Sachs Commodity Index (GSCI), a broad-based index that includes wheat, copper, silver, and natural gas. The index has a fixed weighting by asset class, with the largest target weight of 18% for Brent crude and 18% for gold. Index rebalancing occurs daily to ensure the underlying weights match the stated mandate. These features are standard across similar indices. More granular information on the asset class sub-sectors is available, such as the Bloomberg Cotton Subindex Total Return, which tracks cotton's return.

Commodity indices have some subtle features that differ from equity markets. By comparison, consider the S&P 500 index, which is a market-weighted index of the 500 constituents. This index has just over 500 constituents, because some firms have multiple classes of stock. Therefore, the largest companies have the most weight in the index. What about commodity indices? Does gold deserve more weight than crude oil? Which grade(s) of crude oil? Should weights be based on the dollar-weighted volume of transactions, proven reserves, or some other weighting? Should returns be measured by spot prices or futures prices? As you can see, measuring commodity index returns isn't so simple.

4.12. WHAT STRATEGIES ARE AVAILABLE FOR INVESTING IN COMMODITIES?

Let's return to the fundamental relation between futures prices and spot prices:

Futures price = spot price + costs – benefits, or

Futures price = spot price + cost of carry.

Therefore, if an investor expects the net benefits to be bigger than currently expressed in the market, the investor will go long (buy) the futures contracts. For example, suppose you believe that the upcoming winter is likely to be colder than the current meteorological forecasts. You would want to buy natural gas futures contracts today that expire, say in March.

> "Any commodity that sees its price going higher will see new mines opening up. When the supply increases, the prices soften. When prices fall, some mines with higher production costs will shut down as they become unviable."
> Gautam Adani

As the more frigid winter evolves, you would likely be able to sell futures contracts with March expiry at higher prices due to the high demand for natural gas and close out your original long position for a profit. You also should note the interplay with the storage costs. Due to the colder temperatures, the associated storage costs are low because the long investor won't have to carry (store) the physical commodity until the next winter. The long futures position increases in value by avoiding this drag on returns. You can apply this same logic to many other scenarios, including warmer than expected winters, wheat shortages from a drought, and oversupply of corn from new tariffs or export constraints.

> "Life can be lived at a remove. You trade in futures, and then you trade in derivatives of futures. Banks make more money trading derivatives than they do trading actual commodities."
> Sebastian Faulks

You can also place your funds with a commodity trading advisor (CTA) to execute more complicated trades than just described. A CTA is an individual or firm that advises clients on trading futures, options on futures, swaps, and foreign currencies for a fee and share of profits. Chapter 1 offers a brief discussion of these investments, which are sometimes considered hedge fund strategies. Nevertheless, commodities can be an essential part of a diversified portfolio providing inflation hedging and added diversification. You should generally limit the allocation to a small percentage of your portfolio, such as 5%.

4.13. WHAT MISTAKES SHOULD RETAIL INVESTORS AVOID WHEN INVESTING IN COMMODITIES?

Investors can make mistakes when selecting any investment. Here are some common mistakes to avoid when investing in commodities.

- *Failing to do your homework.* As a first step, you must recognize that commodities are specialized products. You need to become knowledgeable of the specifics involving this alternative asset class and the individual commodity. Thus, you must do your due diligence before investing in commodities, just like any other investment. *Due diligence* is the care and research needed before entering into a proposed transaction with another party.

- *Ignoring measurement error.* You need to be aware that commodity prices behave differently than traditional investments because of their physical nature. Specifically, the return on a futures contract can differ markedly from the return on the underlying commodity. For example, the spot return on crude oil over six months could be 12%, but the futures contract's return, which incorporates transportation and storage, could be, say, a 5% loss. Investors may be accustomed to tracking spot prices and mistakenly expect futures returns to mirror spot returns.

- *Choosing an inappropriate futures contract.* Besides identifying the commodity in which to invest, you must select which futures contract, such as a 1-month, 2-month, or 12-month contract. Making this decision requires thoughtful analysis. For example, the return difference between a February and June expiry can differ based on changing market conditions.

- *Being unprepared for a margin call.* Futures positions require margin. Thus, you must be prepared to meet a sudden margin call. If you don't have the funds to meet the margin call, the CCP will close the position at a loss. Therefore, you may have been on the right side of the trade in the long run, but the short-run financing needs led to a loss. You may not realize the amount of capital needed to meet a margin call and suffer unexpected losses prematurely.

- *Overestimating liquidity.* The physical nature of commodities generally reduces liquidity compared to financial assets. Liquidity can affect both spot prices, futures prices and even widen ETF spreads. Although ETFs are highly liquid, if the underlying commodity markets become illiquid, this change may affect ETF returns. You should realize that illiquidity in the underlying commodities affects the spot, future, and pooled investment returns.

4.14. WHAT ARE SOME ONLINE RESOURCES FOR INVESTING IN COMMODITIES?

Various online resources are available for learning about commodities and commodity investing.

- The CME Group (https://www.cmegroup.com/) has a wealth of information on commodity trading and commodity derivative products.

- The CFTC (https://www.cftc.gov/) provides broad information on regulated futures markets.

- The NFA (https://www.nfa.futures.org/) is a self-regulated registered futures association that promotes best practices for the industry. The NFA provides educational material, industry information as well as requirements for members.

- ETF.com (https://www.etf.com/) has information on virtually all aspects of ETFs.

- Commodity.com (https://www.nfa.futures.org/) provides a history of commodity trading.

TAKEAWAYS

Commodity investing can take many forms from direct ownership, rare for individual investors, to buying shares of companies engaging in mining, refining, modifying, or producing related end products, buying PIVs (mutual funds and ETFs), and trading futures contracts. Although individual commodities may make sense for some investors, they're likely to be a poor investment for most investors. Do-it-yourself investors who don't have specific knowledge about a particular commodity should consider investing in broad commodity funds. However, commodities can play a small part in a diversified portfolio, especially for more experienced and savvy investors. Here are some of this chapter's critical takeaways for individual investors.

- Adopt an investment strategy in commodities that meets your specific needs.

- Avoid investing in commodities if you're a beginner because they're much more complicated than stocks and bonds.

- Avoid buying most physical commodities because you must pay storage, insurance, and other fees.

- Consider buying commodities indirectly through mutual funds and ETFs.

- Consider using commodities as a potential inflation hedge and another source of diversification in your portfolio.

- Analyze the risk-return tradeoff before investing in commodities.

- Be aware that many commodities lack liquidity, so you might not be able to sell at a favorable price.

5

INVESTING IN INFRASTRUCTURE: A ROAD TO ECONOMIC GROWTH

"Infrastructure is the foundation of economic development."
> Craig Lesser, Managing Partner of the Pendleton Consulting Group

You've probably heard the term infrastructure, given its wide use in the media and importance to society. Although the infrastructure asset class is quite broad, *infrastructure* refers to the basic facilities and systems necessary for an economy to function. Today, an enormous need exists for infrastructure investment. Governments worldwide must invest trillions of dollars in maintaining existing infrastructure assets and devote more to building new infrastructure to support economic growth.

> *"Our infrastructure systems are failing to keep pace with current and expanding needs, while investment in infrastructure falters."*
> Carol Haddock

Yet, a considerable gap exists between maintaining and building infrastructure relative to the amount of investment required to meet economic needs and long-term trends. Although federal, state, and local governments have traditionally been responsible for financing public infrastructure, fiscally constrained governments increasingly turn to the private sector to assist in funding new projects. Consequently, the investment opportunities in this sector continue to grow. Because governments cannot meet the global economy's infrastructure requirements on their own, this situation represents a tremendous opportunity for the private sector to play an essential role in building the infrastructure needed to support global growth.

This chapter discusses investing in infrastructure from an individual, not an institutional, investor's perspective. Its primary purpose is to provide the information needed to help you become a savvy investor enabling you to make more informed decisions about investing in infrastructure. This chapter explains the role infrastructure can play as an asset class in your portfolio and how you can invest in infrastructure. Although such investments can occur directly or indirectly, this chapter concentrates on listed infrastructure securities and places little emphasis on unlisted infrastructure private equity (PE) funds. Publicly-traded equity and debt vehicles for investing in infrastructure provide the most attractive route for individual investors.

5.1. WHAT IS INFRASTRUCTURE?

The term infrastructure originated in the late 1880s and was derived from Latin roots "infra-" meaning "below" and "struere" meaning "to build." In fact, some infrastructure is underground, such as sewer systems and natural gas and water supply systems. Although once confined to public works infrastructure, the term has widened to include the internal framework in any technology system or business organization. However, this chapter limits its examination of infrastructure to long-lived assets that pro-

> "We use infrastructure every day, often without noticing."
> Matthew DeLallo

vide public facilities and services, not businesses' infrastructure. Thus, *infrastructure* refers to the physical structures and systems needed to support the economy.

5.2. WHY IS INFRASTRUCTURE NECESSARY?

Infrastructure serves as the foundation for building the structure of the economy. It can lead to faster economic growth and the alleviation of poverty in the country. Not surprisingly, infrastructure often involves high-cost investments essential to a country's economic development and prosperity. Although infrastructure typically operates in the background, economies would cease to function as we know them without infrastructure. Having a deteriorating infrastructure is likely to impede a country's ability to compete in the thriving global economy.

5.3. WHO OWNS INFRASTRUCTURE?

Because large-scale infrastructure often involves producing public goods and services, governments either completely fund or heavily subsidize infrastructure projects. Governments are not only crucial investors, but they also own and operate the most critical infrastructure assets. In the United States, state and local governments, not the federal government, pay for most US infrastructure development and maintenance. Thus, infrastructure investment largely remains a

> "Investment in infrastructure is a long term requirement for growth and a long term factor that will make growth sustainable."
>
> Chanda Kochhar

public sector "business." For example, the US federal government owns Amtrak, which provides passenger train services throughout the country and operates most passenger airports.

Historically, governments generally funded and managed infrastructure. Given that public investments alone can't keep pace with the increasing demand for infrastructure development, private participation in infrastructure (PPI) and public-private partnerships (PPPs) can help bridge the infrastructure financing gap. However, according to a recent World Bank study (https://ppi.worldbank.org/content/dam/PPI/documents/SPIReport_2017_small_interactive.pdf), the share of private investment in infrastructure projects in developing countries remains relatively low. PPIs and PPPs can leverage private capital, expertise, and other benefits to make public dollars go further. Governments have used these models since the early 1990s to finance and procure infrastructure projects around the world. Although governments strapped for cash have turned to these models to build everything from airports to parking garages, private companies express less interest in investing in these types of ventures.

Another trend is for governments to privatize infrastructure assets by selling them to investors. Examples of infrastructure assets moving from public (government) to private (investor) hands include such subsectors as renewable energy, including wind and solar, toll roads, and ports. An example of infrastructure in private hands is the Dulles Greenway toll road in northern Virginia of the United States. Although TRIP II is the concessionaire for Dulles Greenway, Atlas Arteria

Limited (ALX:AU), an Australian company, maintains this toll road. Atlas Arteria is also one of the world's largest developers and operators of private toll roads. It also is an infrastructure developer and operator of highways, roads, bridges, and tunnels. Atlas Arteria Private companies also operate most freight lines in the United States.

> "Across the United States, years of neglect have resulted in crumbling roads, bridges in need of repair, inadequate public transport, outdated school buildings, and other critical infrastructure needs."
> Elizabeth McNichol

Another example is the Chicago Skyway, a 7.8-mile-long toll road connecting the Indiana Toll Road to the Dan Ryan Expressway on Chicago's South Side. Although built by the City of Chicago in 1958, it became the first privatization of an existing toll road in the United States when Skyway Concession Company, LLC assumed its operations under a 99-year operating lease. In February 2016, three Canadian pension funds acquired Skyway. Dozens of US publicly traded-companies own electric and gas utilities.

5.4. WHO INVESTS IN INFRASTRUCTURE OUTSIDE OF GOVERNMENTS?

Infrastructure investing consists of allocating capital to essential facilities and public services that help the economy function and grow and facilitate society's operation. Other than governments, investors in infrastructure include institutional and individual (retail) investors. Demand for infrastructure assets has increased, especially among institutional investors. Such assets provide a good match for defined-benefit pension

> "We've got to move beyond the idea that the public and private sectors are at odds. Government has to lay the groundwork for private equity to productively invest in things like education. It's a partnership, not a battle."
>
> Sebastian Pinera

liabilities, endowment and foundation obligations, large banks, investment arms of insurance companies, and sovereign wealth funds. A *sovereign wealth fund* is a state-owned investment fund that invests in real and financial assets. Institutional investors prefer to access infrastructure investments in two ways: (1) PE-style, unlisted vehicles and (2) direct investing in the assets themselves, either as co-investors with a fund as discussed in Chapter 2 or through outright ownership. Despite the high demand for infrastructure, institutional investors allocate only a small proportion of their assets to infrastructure partly due to the absence of adequate investment benchmarks and associated risks.

Individuals also engage in the funding of public infrastructure. They do so through various indirect investment vehicles that involve publicly-traded infrastructure securities. These securities included common stock, listed mutual funds, exchange-traded funds (ETFs), and master limited partnerships (MLPs). Other investment vehicles are unlisted private-equity funds or "infrastructure funds."

5.5. HOW CAN INFRASTRUCTURE BE CLASSIFIED?

Several ways are available to classify infrastructure, and some of these classification schemes overlap. Each category has several distinguishing characteristics.

- *Types of infrastructure.* Various types of infrastructure are available, including the following:

  - *Transportation.* This category consists of physical assets designed to move people and goods such as road and railway systems, tunnels, bridges, mass-transit systems, seaports, airports, waterways, and canals. Transportation infrastructure assets often operate under a *concession agreement* between a company and the government. The company has the right to operate an asset within the government's jurisdiction and receive its cash flows for a specified period before returning it to the government.

  - *Utilities.* This type of infrastructure includes energy-generating facilities (e.g., gas, electric, wind, and hydro-electric), waste removal, and sanitation facilities.

  - *Energy.* Infrastructure assets in the energy area are in the "midstream" segment of the value chain, such as pipeline companies. These assets typically deal with transporting, processing, or storing commodities such as oil and gas developed by upstream exploration and production companies to deliver to downstream customers, including refiners or utilities.

  - *Communications.* This category of infrastructure consists of broadcast, telephone cable, and mobile-phone systems.

  - *Social.* A final type of infrastructure involves education, health services (e.g., hospitals, clinics, and emergency response systems), law enforcement, and correctional facilities.

- *Hard and soft infrastructure.* The characteristics of hard and soft infrastructure differ.

○ *Hard infrastructure*, also called *economic infrastructure*, refers to the extensive physical facilities and networks needed for a nation to function effectively. These long-lived assets include the four types of infrastructure previously mentioned: transportation, utilities,

> "*Roads remain the essential network of the non-virtual world. They are the infrastructure upon which almost all other infrastructure depends. They are the paths of human endeavor.*"
>
> Ted Conover

energy, and communications. Hard infrastructure usually provides the most infrastructure investment opportunities.

○ *Soft infrastructure* includes those institutions needed to maintain the economy. Some call these institutions *social* as indicated under types of infrastructure.

• *Asset segment*. This approach classifies infrastructure assets based on a risk-return spectrum of a particular sub-sector.

○ *Core and core-plus*. Infrastructure in this asset segment is on the lower end of the risk-return spectrum. Investors earn the majority of their returns from cash yield with limited capital appreciation potential. *Cash yield* is a return measure that estimates the income that an asset generates. Examples of investments in this segment include bridges, tunnels, toll roads, pipelines, energy transmission and distribution, and water and wastewater systems.

○ *Value-added*. Investing in the value-added segment involves greater risk but higher expected returns.

Assets in this segment include airports, seaports, rail links, contracted power generation, and rapid rail transit.

o *Opportunistic.* The opportunistic asset segment includes infrastructure at the higher end of the risk-return spectrum. Such assets include development projects, satellite networks, and merchant power generation. To illustrate this opportunistic segment, let's look at a *merchant power plant*, which is a power plant built or purchased with PE designed for competitive wholesale power marketplaces. Such plants differ from conventional independent power projects, which are regulated power companies that often have near-monopolies in their markets. In contrast, merchant plants don't have upfront, long-term power purchase agreements from firm customers to cover their output. Instead, they generate capacity on a speculative basis and then sell their power at competitive rates to unregulated markets.

o *Geographic location.* Another way to classify investments in infrastructure is by their location.

5.6. WHAT IS THE DIFFERENCE BETWEEN BROWNFIELD AND GREENFIELD INVESTMENTS?

One way to view infrastructure investments is by constructing the assets from scratch or building upon existing assets. A *brownfield investment* involves the upkeep and improvement of existing assets, whereas a *greenfield investment* is an asset to be built. They differ in terms of the predictability in their risk and cash flows.

• *Brownfield investments.* These investments are typically less risky than greenfield investments because they're mature assets with long operating histories. As a result, they tend to provide more stable cash flows but lower returns commensurate with their lower risk. Their overall returns consist of a higher cash yield but relatively little growth potential.

- *Greenfield investments.* In contrast, greenfield investments are infrastructure assets to be constructed. Thus, they face more significant uncertainty due to *completion risk* resulting from such factors as construction and bureaucratic delays, cost over-runs, and deadline commitments. Similarly, *usage risk* results from insufficient demand for the service provided by the greenfield investment once built. As a result, investors could experience lower than expected returns and potential bankruptcy in extreme cases. Although greenfield investments may initially have a lower income component (i.e., lower cash yield) than brownfield investments due to higher reinvestment requirements and low cash flow, they offer more growth potential.

To avoid greenfield investment risks, you can invest in existing infrastructure (brownfield investments) with stable operating histories or funds focused on replacing existing assets. However, you're likely to be compensated with higher returns if you're willing to take the added risks associated with greenfield investments.

5.7. WHAT ARE THE COMMON ATTRIBUTES OF INFRASTRUCTURE INVESTMENTS?

According to the typical infrastructure-investment narrative, infrastructure assets uniquely combine several characteristics to make them attractive investments.

- *Essential to society or the economy.* By engaging in infrastructure investing, you can allocate capital to tangible assets to provide services critical to society and facilitate the economy's overall functioning and growth. These assets often offer an attractive investment opportunity because of their essential nature.

- *Long lives and high costs.* Infrastructure assets typically have long, useful lives and require much upfront capital to build and maintain, making replication difficult due to construction costs and scarcity of resources.

- *Regulation.* Many infrastructure assets operate in a regulated environment. Consequently, a government entity often provides a regulated return on invested capital. In other instances, contracts govern infrastructure assets, such as in concession or contracted assets.

- *Monopoly-like market position.* Such assets often occupy a monopoly/quasi-monopoly market position or have high barriers to entry. Due to limited competition, infrastructure project companies have pricing power subject to constraints established by regulators.

- *Resistance to business cyclicality.* Because infrastructure assets generally have monopolistic positions and provide essential services in the areas in which they operate, the demand for these services is relatively insensitive to economic weakness and price increases. For example, consumers still need electricity and water despite higher prices.

> *"Quality infrastructure is positively related to effective global value chains, efficient economies and better living standards."*
> World Economic Forum

- *Predictable and sustainable free cash flow.* Compared to other investments, infrastructure, especially "core" infrastructure investments, can produce relatively steady free cash flows with a healthy yield component. These stable cash flows result from low volatility (risk). *Free cash flow* is the cash a company produces through its operations, less the cost of expenditures on assets, available to distribute to all of its securities holders such as bondholders and shareholders.

- *Liquidity issues. Liquidity* refers to the ease of trading a security. Compared to other assets, infrastructure can be less liquid due to the higher costs of these assets and the limited number of potential buyers. Investments in unlisted infrastructure PE funds have lower liquidity due to their legal structure and restrictions. Investors can't liquidate their partnership interests without a transaction on the secondary market, which involves a high risk of loss due to selling partnership interests at a discount on the reported net asset value. The deep discount is because the secondary market is in its infancy resulting in fewer trading opportunities. However, investors can enhance their liquidity based on the type of vehicle through which they gain infrastructure exposure. For example, investing in listed securities such as mutual funds, ETFs, or MLPs that invest in infrastructure assets can lessen liquidity and capital market risks while providing investors with exposure to this alternative asset class.

5.8. WHY CONSIDER INVESTING IN INFRASTRUCTURE?

Investing in infrastructure can benefit both investors and society. From a societal perspective, investment in infrastructure fuels economic growth, can result in a more productive economy, spur job growth, improve the quality of life, and lead to a better environment. Although infrastructure doesn't represent the "sexy part" of any portfolio, its unique characteristics offer investors several potential benefits.

- *Diversification.* Investing in infrastructure provides good diversification benefits to investors' portfolios. Why? Its returns have low correlations with the business cycle and other asset classes due to the relatively consistent demand and inherent inflation protection characteristics of infrastructure assets. Being less correlated with ongoing fluctuations of financial markets or the overall economy offers the possibility of improving portfolio diversification and a portfolio's risk-return characteristics.

  Additionally, having a range of infrastructure investment vehicles is particularly attractive, given that markets in traditional investments continue to become more correlated. Individual investors can use investments in infrastructure to counterbalance broadly indexed listed investments such as stocks. Consequently, they tend to invest in infrastructure funds for their defensive characteristics to help combat volatility, such as funds engaging in transportation or water infrastructure. However, keep in mind that diversification can lessen but not eliminate the risk of loss.

- *Attractive risk-adjusted returns.* Historically, infrastructure investments have offered attractive risk-adjusted returns. Infrastructure companies typically operate in environments where the buyer's demand doesn't

"Many investment experts agree that infrastructure is a very lucrative area for investment."

Brian J. Block

change much relative to the price changes. Additionally, infrastructure is subject to high levels of regulation or contracting. As an asset class, infrastructure tends to produce lower returns and volatility than equities over long-term periods but provides a better yield than government debt. Governments are aware that private owners must earn fair returns to incentivize them to invest in infrastructure. Although infrastructure investors primarily focus on preserving value and generating current income, potential capital appreciation is available, especially when investing in opportunistic infrastructure assets. Returns tend to differ based on not only asset segment with expected returns increasing from core and core-plus to value-added, and then to opportunistic segments, but also where the assets are domiciled and their legal jurisdiction.

- *Stable cash flows and economic insensitivity.* Infrastructure assets provide essential services and generally occupy monopolistic positions, meaning that they have little competition. As a result, their demand tends to be reasonably stable. Such economic insensitivity leads to generating long-term, stable cash flows because users don't substantially reduce usage during periods of economic weakness or after rate increases. However, keep in mind that some infrastructure investments seek to distribute income, such as the core and core-plus asset segments. Others are more focused on long-term total returns, specifically the value-added and opportunistic asset segments.

- *Potential inflation hedge.* A link often exists between infrastructure assets performance and macro indicators such as inflation, gross domestic product, and population growth. Consequently, many investors view infrastructure as a hedge. For example, infrastructure assets can offer some inflation protection as a result of their remuneration structures. That is, these structures link the rates charged for using infrastructure assets to inflation. Regulators, concession agreements for PPPs, and long-term contracts that take inflation into account determine these rates. For example, companies are allowed a "real" return on invested capital plus explicit compensation for inflation in regulated and contracted infra-structure. In other situations, owners of infrastructure assets can pass inflation on to consumers through price increases, given the assets' essential nature and their inelastic demand.

> *"Infrastructure returns will ultimately be impacted by the frequency, intensity and complexity of asymmetric risks."*
> Jeffrey Altman

5.9. WHAT ARE THE POTENTIAL RISKS ASSOCIATED WITH INVESTING IN INFRASTRUCTURE?

A basic tenet of infrastructure investment is that investors enjoy a risk-return balance between downside protection and upside return potential. Since the early 2010s, the risk-return balance has proven somewhat lopsided or asymmetrical for many investors due to the frequency, intensity, and complexity of various risks. Thus, investing in infrastructure involves several risks. *Infrastructure risk* is the potential for losses due to failures of essential services, organizational structures, and facilities.

Some of these risks are mainly within the control of investors and managers (*endogenous risks*), while others are outside of their control (*exogenous risks*). For example, investors can partially control their risk level by selecting

> *"The key problem with infrastructure spending is that it almost always attaches risk onto taxpayers that should fall on the private sector, which takes cost overruns more seriously."*
>
> William Murray

infrastructure investments based on their development stage (brownfield or greenfield investments) or asset segment (core and core-plus, value-added, and opportunistic). Additionally, given the relatively low correlations among infrastructure sub-sectors, you can create a well-diversified infrastructure portfolio to reduce your risk. Private owners who own and operate infrastructure can control operational risk and cost overruns. Still, they can't control government involvement, a rise in interest rates, and access to capital to fund infrastructure projects. Today, endogenous (internal) risks may be more dangerous because they're difficult to anticipate or control. Here are several critical risks of infrastructure investing.

- *Political, regulatory, and currency risk*. Investors face *political risk* when political decisions, events, or conditions substantially affect a business' profitability or an organization's effectiveness. They encounter *regulatory risk* when changes in laws and regulations materially affect a business or an organization. Both types of risk can influence an investment's expected return. The political and regulatory environment varies substantially from one country or region to another. Such differences increase both the complexity of investing in infrastructure and the uncertainty for investors. Investors can mitigate political and regulatory risk by understanding the political, regulatory, and legal environments where they are investing. Investing in politically stable regions with established legal and regulatory frameworks such as the United States can also reduce such risks. Another way to moderate these risks is to use a global infrastructure investment strategy to provide diversification benefits. However, this latter approach can lead to *currency risk*, which is the potential risk of loss from fluctuating foreign exchange rates when an investor has exposure to foreign currency or in foreign-currency-traded investments.

- *Environmental and social risk. Environmental and social (E&S) risks* are the potential negative consequences to a business resulting from its real or perceived impact on the environment or community. Environmental risks in infrastructure projects can occur both at the construction phase and during operations. Such risks often include environmental pollution, hazards to human health, safety and security, and threats to a region's biodiversity. The inability to effectively manage E&S issues can have financial, legal, or reputational consequences. For example, environmentalism affects every infrastructure sector, leading to stricter standards for air, land, water quality, and waste management, which can require a massive infusion of capital into new and existing facilities.

- *Technological risk. Technological risk* is the risk of implementing new technology that causes adverse impacts on its business processes or mission. Technological innovation can have a dramatic effect on the infrastructure industry and investment returns. Emerging technologies offer both promises and pitfalls. Adopting advancing technologies can result in improved efficiency, greater market opportunities, and better returns on investment. Yet, such adoption can potentially disrupt all types of infrastructure, potentially derail or destroy an otherwise compelling project, and require substantial capital outlays.

5.10. HOW CAN INVESTORS GAIN EXPOSURE TO INFRASTRUCTURE?

Infrastructure investing involves allocating capital to tangible assets that deliver essential services to society and help the economy function and grow. Investors can gain exposure to infrastructure, either directly or indirectly. Investors get direct exposure through private markets by owning the companies that build or operate the infrastructure assets or engaging in a PPP. With this approach, investors face all the risks associated with infrastructure investments. In contrast, investors can gain indirect exposure to infrastructure through publicly listed companies whose business is directly related to infrastructure assets. They can also buy municipal bonds. In the United States, the municipal bond market is the primary means of financing public infrastructure. For most investors in infrastructure, indirect investment is more practical because it involves more benefits – such as liquidity and transparency – with relatively few drawbacks.

5.11. WHAT ARE PUBLICLY-TRADED VEHICLES AVAILABLE FOR INVESTING IN INFRASTRUCTURE?

Individual investors have several ways to invest in infrastructure through listed equity and debt vehicles. However, exchange-traded equity vehicles constitute only part of the overall universe of infrastructure investments. Additionally, a concentration of these investments occurs in a few asset categories. The major types of publicly-traded equity investment vehicles in infrastructure are stocks, mutual funds, ETFs, and MLPs. Yet, debt, such as municipals bonds, is used to finance about 90% of state and local capital infrastructure spending.

5.12. WHAT ARE THE PROS AND CONS OF INVESTING IN INFRASTRUCTURE STOCKS?

Common stock is a type of equity share issued by a corporation or entity. As a shareholder, you're a proportionate owner of an entity. *Infrastructure stocks* refer to companies that own and operate hard infrastructure assets. Investing in listed infrastructure stocks involves both pros and cons. On the positive side, infrastructure stocks offer attractive long-term returns through cash dividends and potential capital appreciation, which provides one of the best ways to stay ahead of inflation. The amount of the dividend relative to the share price is called the *dividend yield*.

However, as previously indicated, different asset segments – core and core-plus, value-added, and opportunistic – offer different risk levels and returns. You can also use infrastructure stocks to diversify your portfolio to reduce risk or volatility over time. Publicly-traded infrastructure stocks

> *"Buying a company without having sufficient knowledge of it may be even more dangerous than having inadequate diversification."*
>
> Philip Fisher

are highly liquid, meaning you can quickly sell your holdings. Finally, buying or selling these stocks involves low transaction costs.

On the negative side, infrastructure stocks make no promises of future returns. Although the stock market can be unpredictable, core and core-plus infrastructure stocks typically have relatively higher and sustainable cash flows independent of market movements, making them more defensive than stocks in general. However, the coronavirus pandemic decimated corporate America and the broader economy in

2020, leading US businesses, including those involved in infrastructure, to cut or suspend dividends. Thus, the economic slump sparked by the coronavirus outbreak has imperiled a popular investment strategy of buying dividend stocks.

5.13. WHAT ARE SOME EXAMPLES OF INFRASTRUCTURE STOCKS?

Numerous infrastructure stocks are available around the world (https://www.value.today/world-top-companies/infrastructure). Crunchbase.com lists 881 organizations in the infrastructure space in the United States (https://www.crunchbase.com/hub/united-states-infrastructure-companies#section-overview). Macquarie Infrastructure Corporation (NYSE: MIC) owns, operates, and invests in a portfolio of infrastructure and infrastructure-like businesses in the United States. Nucor Corporation (NYSE: NUE) is an American producer of steel and related products that often play a role in infrastructure projects.

Companies are also involved in other aspects of the infrastructure industry. Caterpillar (NYSE: CAT), the construction-machinery maker, is a quintessential infrastructure play. Vulcan Materials (NYSE: VMC) produces and sells construction aggregates, asphalt mix, and ready-mixed concrete, primarily in the United States for highways, airports, and government buildings. Martin Marietta Materials (NYSE: MLM), an aggregates and building materials supplier, sells products required for bridge and road projects. Aecom (NYSE: ACM) is a full-service design, engineering, and construction company that operates worldwide. The company handles planning, engineering, design, program management, and construction management for clients.

Examples of stocks in hard infrastructure include the following:

- *Transportation* (airports, toll roads, ports, and railroads). For example, Transurban Group (OTC US: TRAUF) owns and operates toll road networks in Australia and North American. Norfolk Southern Railway (NYSE: NSC) is a Class I freight railroad in the United States and one of the nation's premier transportation companies. Investors in railroad stocks, such as Norfolk Southern, BNSF (a subsidiary of Berkshire Hathaway), Union Pacific Corporation (NYSE: UPC), and CSX (NASDAQ: CSX), often hold them for their long-term income stream.

- *Utilities* (electricity transmission and distribution, natural gas distribution, water, and renewables). Many view utility stocks as a safe investment to add to a portfolio because they're part of a regulated industry and often have few competitors. The largest publicly-traded US energy utilities are Pacific Gas and Electric Company (PG&E) (NYSE: PCG). Others include Southern California Edison, a subsidiary of Edison International (NYSE: EIX), Commonwealth Edison Co, a subsidiary of Exelon Corporation (NASDAQ: EXC), and Consolidated Edison Co (NYSE: ED). NextEra Inc (NYSE: NEE) is the largest electric utility holding company by market capitalization and a leading clean energy (e.g., solar and wind) company. Other top US energy companies are Duke Energy (NYSE: DUK) and Dominion Energy (NYSE: D). American Water Works Co Inc (NYSE: AWK) is the largest water utility in the United States, providing water, wastewater, and other services to residential, commercial, and industrial customers in the United States and Canada.

- *Energy* (pipeline companies and oil and gas midstream). The United States has more midstream energy infrastructure than all other countries combined. Kinder Morgan, Inc .(NYSE: KMI) is North America's leading gas infrastructure company, followed by Williams Companies (NYSE: WMB), a major natural gas pipeline operator. Canada's Enbridge (NYSE: ENB), the largest energy infrastructure company in North America, operates the world's longest crude oil and liquids transportation system. Another Canadian company is TC Energy (NYSE: TRP), one of North America's largest gas pipeline companies. Historically, much of the midstream space has been structured as MLPs, as discussed later.

- *Communications* (wireless towers and fixed orbit satellite operators). American Tower Corporation (NYSE: AMT) is an American real estate investment trust (REIT) and an owner and operator of wireless and broadcast communications infrastructure in several countries worldwide. Crown Castle (NYSE: CCI) is a REIT and the largest provider of shared communications infrastructure (cell towers) in the United States.

5.14. WHY ARE MUTUAL FUNDS AN ATTRACTIVE VEHICLE FOR INVESTING IN INFRASTRUCTURE?

A problem facing investors in infrastructure stocks is selecting which individual stocks to include in a portfolio. Many individual investors have neither the time nor expertise to engage in this task. Therefore, they choose to invest in a pooled investment vehicle such as a mutual fund or an ETF.

A *mutual fund* is an open-end investment fund that pools money from various investors to buy securities. These funds offer diversification, professional management, and ease of investing in specialized sectors. The low minimum requirements for most mutual funds enable you to invest frequently.

You can directly buy infrastructure mutual funds from a mutual fund company, such as Fidelity, a bank and a brokerage firm. Before you can start investing, you'll need to have an account with one of these institutions before placing an order.

Two types of management are available for mutual funds: active and passive. Active management requires frequent buying and selling to outperform a specific benchmark or index. As a result, it involves greater risks and entails larger fees. In contrast, passive management endeavors to replicate or mirror a particular benchmark or index to match its performance. Thus, passively managed funds try to "meet" the market, not "beat" the market.

5.15. WHAT ARE SOME EXAMPLES OF INFRASTRUCTURE MUTUAL FUNDS?

Infrastructure funds offer the opportunity to invest in essential public assets. Industries considered to be part of the infrastructure sector include airports, integrated shipping, railroads, shipping and ports, trucking, oil and gas midstream, waste management, engineering and construction, infrastructure operations, and the utility sector. Here are four actively managed infrastructure mutual funds with varying characteristics (https://money.usnews .com/funds/mutual-funds/rankings/infrastructure). Each of these infrastructure equity funds typically invests at least 80% of its assets in stocks of companies engaged in infrastructure activities.

- *Frontier MFG Core Infrastructure Fund (FMGIX).* This fund's goal is long-term capital appreciation by concentrating in the infrastructure sector – regulated energy and water utilities, toll roads, airports, ports, communications infrastructure, and social infrastructure. This no-load fund has low fees but requires a minimum of $100,000 investment.

• *Lazard Global Listed Infrastructure Portfolio (GLIFX)*. This actively managed portfolio seeks long-term, defensive, low-volatility returns that exceed inflation by investing in equity securities of infrastructure companies with a minimum market capitalization of $250 million. The securities in these infrastructure companies are listed on a national or other recognized securities exchange. This no-load fund charges average fees and requires a $10,000 initial investment.

• *Nuveen Global Infrastructure Fund (FGNCX)*. This fund has a total return focus. It seeks long-term growth of capital and income from global economic development by investing in infrastructure companies that own or operate vital structures, facilities, and services. The fund diversifies its investments among different countries worldwide, including equity securities of emerging market issuers. This load fund charges a 1% load, has a moderate fee level, and requires a $3,000 minimum initial investment.

> *"Mutual funds have historically offered safety and diversification. And they spare you the responsibility of picking individual stocks."*
>
> Ron Chernow

A *load fund* is a mutual fund that has a sales charge or commission. If you invest in this fund, you pay the load, which compensates a sales intermediary, such as a broker, financial planner, or investment advisor, for assistance and advice in selecting an appropriate fund

- *JHancock Infrastructure Fund (JEEBX)*. The fund's objective is to seek total return from capital appreciation and income by investing its net assets in global securities of companies with infrastructure-related assets. This actively managed fund aims to outperform global equities over a complete market cycle, focusing on limiting losses in flat or negative markets. Its primary use is for managing downside risk and a potential inflation hedge. It targets companies with long-lived physical assets and revenue streams that may benefit from contractual inflation adjustments to manage downside risk. These companies often pay attractive dividends, which the fund generally distributes quarterly. This fund charges a 5% load, has a moderate fee level, and requires a minimum initial investment of $1,000.

5.16. HOW CAN INVESTORS CHOOSE BETWEEN DIFFERENT TYPES OF INFRASTRUCTURE MUTUAL FUNDS?

If you are considering investing in infrastructure mutual funds, you should consider several factors before investing.

- *Risk-return profile.* The type of asset that an infrastructure fund holds affects its risk-return profile. You want to make sure that a fund's objective matches your own. An excellent place to start is to familiarize yourself with a fund's *prospectus*, a document detailing the fund's goals and strategies, and providing specifics on the fund's past performance and managers.

- *Cost.* You should pay close attention to a fund's after-cost returns because a small difference in fees and expenses can translate into substantial differences in returns over time. Where possible, you should avoid funds with fees, called load funds, because similar no-load funds are often available.

- *Potential performance.* You may have come across the disclaimer that "past performance is not indicative of future results." This warning is not only sound advice, but it's also the law. The Securities and Exchange Commission (SEC) Rule 156 requires mutual funds to inform investors not to base their future performance expectations on past performance before investing. You want to avoid chasing past performance. Nonetheless, reviewing a fund's past performance may help you better understand its investment philosophy and style. When examining performance, you should take a long view of how a fund performed during different phases of the market cycle.

- *Fund management.* The fund manager directly affects a fund's performance. You should become familiar with fund managers, including their strategy, experience, and consistency in generating strong returns. A fund's prospectus typically discloses these factors.

- *Diversification.* You should consider a mutual fund's diversification benefits, but they differ among funds. Some are likely to provide more diversification benefits than others by investing in different types of infrastructure.

5.17. WHY ARE ETFS A GOOD INVESTMENT VEHICLE FOR INFRASTRUCTURE?

An *ETF* is a basket of securities whose shares trade on an exchange throughout the day, just like a typical stock. ETFs provide a convenient way to obtain low-cost portfolio diversification and segment exposure. Passively managed (index) ETFs typically have lower expenses than actively managed

ETFs. Additionally, ETFs offer transparency by disclosing their holdings on a regular and frequent basis, so you know each fund's assets. Unlike mutual funds, you can buy or sell ETFs throughout the trading day, which provides intraday trading liquidity. Based on their structure, ETFs are tax-efficient because you only realize capital gains and losses when selling an ETF. The ongoing need for new roads, bridges, expressways, tunnels, and other infrastructure types can make infrastructure ETFs attractive.

> "ETF portfolios will be the inevitable default for investors in the years to come because they are lower cost, more transparent and offer greater liquidity and tax advantages than mutual funds."
>
> Jon Stein

> "If you have the stomach for stocks, but neither the time nor the inclination to do the homework, invest in equity mutual funds."
>
> Peter Lynch

5.18. WHAT BENCHMARKS ARE AVAILABLE FOR PUBLICLY LISTED INFRASTRUCTURE SECURITIES?

Many benchmarks are available for measuring indexed mutual funds and ETFs investing in infrastructure. Constructing most of these indices involves applying a market-cap-weighting methodology to infrastructure sectors or imposing hard caps (i.e., specified maximum percentages) on these sectors. In benchmarking, the publicly listed infrastructure market, S&P Dow Jones Indices have been a leader, but others in this space also offer indices such as MSCI, Macquarie, and FTSE.

- *Dow Jones Brookfield Global Infrastructure Composite (DJBGI) Index* consists of companies domiciled globally that qualify as "pure-play" *infrastructure companies*. These companies must obtain at least 70% of their cash flows from owning and operating infrastructure assets.

- *S&P Global Infrastructure Index* tracks 75 global companies chosen to represent the listed infrastructure industry. It creates diversified exposure by including three distinct infrastructure clusters: energy, transportation, and utilities.

- *MSCI ACWI Infrastructure Index*. With 261 components, this index captures the global opportunity set of companies that are owners or operators of infrastructure assets. The index provides broad-based infrastructure exposure but is heavily weighted (> 90%) in the telecommunications and utility sectors.

- *Macquarie Global Infrastructure 100 Index* reflects companies' stock performance within the infrastructure industry, mainly those engaged in management, ownership, and operation of infrastructure and utility assets.

- *FTSE Global Core Infrastructure 50/50 Index* offers broad-based, utilities-centric exposure with 50% in utilities, 30% in transportation, and a 20% mix of other sectors, including pipelines, satellites, and telecommunication towers.

5.19. WHAT ARE SOME EXAMPLES OF INFRASTRUCTURE ETFS?

Although you can't invest directly in an index, you can invest in an index ETF, which seeks to replicate and track a benchmark index as closely as possible. Here are a few examples of passively managed (index) ETFs focusing on infrastructure.

- *ProShares DJ Brookfield Global Infrastructure ETF (TOLZ)* seeks investment results, before fees and expenses, that track the DJBGI Index's performance. TOLZ is the only ETF that offers pure-play exposure.

> "When you own an index fund, you're also protected against all the downright dumb, mildly misguided or merely unlucky decisions that active fund managers are liable to make."
>
> Tony Robbins

- *iShares US Infrastructure ETF* (BATS: IFRA) seeks to track the investment results of the NYSE® FactSet US Infrastructure Index.

- *SPDR® S&P Global Infrastructure ETF* (GII) seeks results that, before fees and expenses, generally correspond to the total return performance of the S&P Global Infrastructure Index.

- *iShares Global Infrastructure ETF (IGF)* is the biggest, oldest, and most liquid in the infrastructure category, also tracks the S&P Global Infrastructure Index. This fund offers little exposure to emerging markets, which means that it provides more stability but less growth opportunity than a fund allocating more of its funds to emerging market securities.

5.20. WHAT SELECTION CRITERIA SHOULD INVESTORS USE BEFORE BUYING AN INFRASTRUCTURE ETF?

If you're considering buying an infrastructure ETF, it should be consistent with your investment plan, including your objectives and risk tolerance. You need to be aware of what the ETF tracks if it's an index fund, how it's constructed, the securities held, how long the ETF has been around, and the tax consequences of owning the fund. Here are some specific selection criteria.

- *Underlying index.* Infrastructure ETFs typically track a specific index, and the composition of these indices varies. Because different benchmarks may be suitable for different investments, you want to ensure that the index meets your risk-return objectives.

- *Tracking error. Tracking error* is how closely an ETF tracks its benchmark. ETFs with a good tracking record have a low tracking error and are usually better to buy than those with poor tracking records. Why? An ETF with a high tracking error may indicate a poorly managed fund. Thus, the best or most efficient ETFs tend to closely track the indexes on which they're based and are hence "well-run."

- *Assets under management (AUM).* Although the biggest ETFs aren't always the best to buy, high AUM often translates into high trading volume, high shareholder confidence, low expense ratios (cost), and a long history. These qualities contribute to making the best ETFs.

- *Expenses.* Expenses negatively affect returns. Low and predictable investment costs are important when considering which ETF to buy. Begin by reviewing the fund's *expense ratio,* including management expenses and other administrative expenses involved in the fund's operation, and its pattern and trend. Generally speaking, the lower the expense ratio, the better. Keep in mind that the expense ratio doesn't include such costs as brokerage commissions for buying and selling ETF shares. Because the expense ratio gives a false impression of an ETF's actual costs, you should be concerned with the total cost of ownership. Given that most ETFs passively track a benchmark index, the best ETFs should have a low total ownership cost.

- *Other considerations.* ETFs should provide complete, accurate information in their prospectuses and marketing materials, enabling you to understand their structure, composition, performance, and risks. These funds should also lack any hidden risk. Finally, the best funds also offer the lowest tax exposure for the investment objective and are thus more tax efficient.

5.21. WHAT IS AN MLP?

An *MLP* is a publicly-traded partnership organized primarily for tax purposes. Unlike corporations, MLPs pay no federal income tax at the company level. Thus, MLPs help finance the expansion of the nation's domestic energy infrastructure without government spending and pave the way toward US energy independence and security.

> "*Nearly 90% of all MLPs are in the midstream energy infrastructure services or natural resources sectors.*"
>
> Master Limited Partnership Association (MLPA)

Apache (NYSE: APA), an oil and gas producer, formed the first MLP in 1981. In 1987, the US Congress decided to limit their use to the real estate and natural resources sectors. In 2008, however, Congress expanded this definition of eligible activities to include the storage and transportation of renewable and alternative fuels, including ethanol and biodiesel. However, most MLPs are in the energy sector because of the qualifying income limitations.

The "typical" MLP is an organization involved in the midstream energy industry, including transportation, processing, and storage of oil, natural gas, and natural gas liquids. Pipelines are part of midstream energy infrastructure.

Pipelines serve as a bridge between *upstream companies*, which extract crude oil and natural gas from the ground, and *downstream companies*, which refine and process those raw materials into various fuels and petrochemicals. MLPs don't own these resources but instead receive a set fee for each barrel of oil or million British Thermal Unit (MMBtu) of natural gas transported, stored, or processed in the case of natural gas.

5.22. HOW IS AN MLP STRUCTURED?

As publicly-traded partnerships, MLPs consist of two classes of partners. General partners (GPs), who manage the MLP's operations and receive compensation for its performance, own a small stake in the partnership, usually about 2%. Limited partners (LPs) provide most of the capital and periodically receive a share of the MLP's income, deductions, losses, and credits. A share of an MLP is called a *unit*. Investors in an MLP are *unitholders* instead of shareholders as in a corporation. The units of the LPs trade on the New York Stock Exchange (NYSE) and the Nasdaq Stock Market, as well as many regional exchanges, but those of the GPs usually don't.

An MLP has a hybrid legal structure combining elements of both a partnership and a corporation. Unlike a corporation, which is a legal entity, an MLP is the aggregate of its partners. Thus, MLP investors are LPs in the MLP, not shareholders. Unlike corporations that pay dividends to investors in their common stock. MLPs pay cash distributions to their partners. Like a partnership, an MLP has a pass-through tax structure in which profits and losses flow through to the LPs. The money passed through from the MLP to unitholders is either a return of capital or ordinary income. Typically, about 80%–90% of MLPs distributions are a *return of capital*, which are tax-sheltered distributions, so the unitholder avoids paying income tax on the returns. A return of capital isn't technically income but represents an MLP returning a portion of its assets to unitholders. This exemption from federal corporate taxes due to their structure is a distinct advantage of MLPs. Thus, unitholders enjoy tax deferral on most earnings until they sell their units. They pay taxes at the lower capital gains tax rate instead of the higher personal income rate. This categorization offers substantial additional tax benefits. To maintain pass-through status requires that at least 90% of the MLP's income must be qualifying income realized from the exploration, production, or transportation of natural resources or real estate.

5.23. WHAT WAYS ARE AVAILABLE FOR INVESTING IN AN MLP?

Three ways are available for investing in MLPs. The first way is to invest in units of individual publicly-traded MLPs. Another approach is to buy an MLP mutual fund such as Goldman Sachs MLP Energy Infrastructure Fund (GLPIX) or ETF such as Alerian MLP ETF (NYSEArca: AMLP). A third approach is to invest in an MLP *exchange-traded note* (ETN), an unsecured debt instrument that pays a return linked to a specified index's performance. An example of an MLP ETN is JPMorgan Alerian MLP Index (AMJ). The ETN structure eliminates tracking errors and provides some favorable tax treatment. Specifically, in the United States, ETNs eliminate the need for investors to deal with K-1 reporting documents. As a drawback, ETNs expose investors to the possibility of a total loss if the backing institution goes bankrupt.

5.24. WHAT ARE SOME PROS AND CONS OF INVESTING IN MLPS?

MLPs have both benefits and drawbacks.

- *Benefits*. On the upside, MLPs can be an excellent option for some investors. They offer substantial diversification versus other asset classes. For example, MLPs have either a near-zero or negative correlation to corporate bonds, government bonds, and gold. MLPs also provide steady income, often resulting from long-term service contracts (5–20 years) with low risk. However, MLPs distributions aren't guaranteed. Because MLPs provide attractive yields relative to stocks and bonds, they're appealing to income investors. These cash distributions usually grow at a higher rate than inflation, which can provide an inflation hedge.

  > *"While master limited partnerships can be confusing come tax time, the benefits of high current income and tax deferral outweigh these headaches."*
  > Jared Cummans

  Additionally, MLPs combine the tax benefits of limited partnerships – both tax-advantaged and tax-deferred income – with the liquidity and affordability that publicly-traded securities offer. Finally, using MLPs for estate planning provides tax benefits when unitholders gift or transfer the MLP units to beneficiaries. In summary, MLPs are low-risk, long-term investments that offer a slow but steady income stream.

  > *"Since MLPs widely offer high yields, they are naturally appealing for income investors."*
  > Bob Ciura

- *Drawbacks.* On the downside, MLPs involve complicated tax filing, especially the Schedule K-1. To avoid the tax issues associated with MLPs, you can invest in either a taxable corporation, mutual fund, or ETF that owns MLPs. Tax issues with MLPs can deter investors from holding them in an Individual Retirement Account (IRA) or 401(k). However, if kept in a retirement account, MLPs potentially involve additional paperwork. Another cons associated with MLPs is that they typically offer limited appreciation. Some MLPs have delivered poor investment performance due to mismanagement, oil price volatility, and other reasons. Because MLPs give access mainly to the midstream energy sectors, they provide little diversification within the MLP asset class. However, some non-midstream energy MLPs are available in real estate and other businesses. Given that MLPs typically distribute most of their cash flows to avoid taxes, additional capital usually comes through debt and share issuances. Finally, as with any investment, MLPs involve risks such as legislative risk, environmental risk, permitting risk, and interest rate risk.

5.25. WHAT ARE SOME EXAMPLES OF THE LARGEST AND MOST POPULAR MLP STOCKS?

The concentration of MLP stocks occurs mainly in midstream energy infrastructure or pipelines. Below are some of the largest MLP stocks based on *market capitalization (market cap)*, which refers to the total dollar market value of a company's outstanding stock shares.

- *Energy Transfer* (NYSE: ET). Energy Transfer, the largest, most diversified MLP, operates a fully integrated midstream

platform. Its diversified and fee-based assets provide the
company with a steady cash flow, even during declining oil
and gas prices.

- *Magellan Midstream Partners* (NYSE: MMP).
  Headquartered in Tulsa, Oklahoma, MMP engages in
  the transportation, storage, and distribution of refined
  petroleum products and crude oil in the United States. It
  has the longest pipeline system of refined products in the
  United States.

- *Enterprise Products Partners* (NYSE: EPD). This MLP
  is one of the largest midstream oil and gas companies in
  North America.

- *Brookfield Infrastructure Partners* (NYSE: BIP).
  Headquartered in Toronto, Canada, BIP is one of the
  largest owners and operators of critical and diverse global
  infrastructure networks, facilitating the movement and
  storage of energy, water, freight, passengers, and data.

5.26. WHAT FACTORS SHOULD INVESTORS CONSIDER BEFORE INVESTING IN AN MLP?

When selecting an MLP, you should consider the following
qualities.

- *Predictable cash flow*. The stability of cash flow is a
  characteristic of top-performing MLPs. Such steadiness
  results from long-term fixed-fee contracts and regulated
  rates. Most of an MLP's cash flows should come from
  predictable sources.

- *Conservative distribution coverage ratio*. This metric
  measures the number of times an MLP can cover its current

distribution to investors with cash flow. Although coverage ratios may change over time, you should generally look for MLPs with a conservative coverage ratio of at least 1.5 times cash flow.

- *Strong financial profile.* A strong financial profile is another characteristic of attractive MLPs. For example, they should have an investment-grade credit rating and a low leverage ratio, both of which enable borrowing money at a lower cost.

- *A high-quality portfolio with clear growth prospects.* Another potential screen is to look for MLPs with high-quality assets in the best markets. Having a strong strategic asset footprint is likely to result in demand remaining high, enhancing MLP's ability to expand its asset base and increase its cash flow and distribution.

5.27. WHAT IS AN INFRASTRUCTURE PE FUND?

An infrastructure PE fund is an unlisted investment vehicle designed to attract private financial capital for large infrastructure assets from accredited investors. The investment community views infrastructure PE as distinct from traditional PE because of the infrastructure's distinctive characteristics. These funds may invest in any asset segment – core and core-plus, value-added, and opportunistic. For example, Global Infrastructure Partners (GIP), headquartered in New York, is a leading global infrastructure investment fund making equity and selected debt investments. Its equity investments are in infrastructure assets in the energy, transport, and water/waste sectors.

Various infrastructure PE firms invest mainly in core infrastructure. For instance, Amber Infrastructure Group (Amber), headquartered in London, is a leading international infrastructure specialist, providing asset management and investment advisory services. Amber has sourced, developed, and financed more than 125 social infrastructure, transportation, renewable energy, and urban redevelopment projects across the United Kingdom, Europe, Canada, and Australia. Amber is a global investment manager focused on infrastructure and real estate. Another example is InfraRed Capital Partners, a leading global investment manager focused on infrastructure and real estate. The firm specializes in developing, acquiring, and managing projects from their conception, structuring, and construction to their long-term operating phase. Chapter 2 contains additional information on PE.

5.28. WHAT TYPES OF MUNICIPAL DEBT ARE AVAILABLE FOR INVESTORS INTERESTED IN INVESTING IN INFRASTRUCTURE?

Users, via charges such as tolls, user fees, and utility rates, governments, mainly through taxes and borrowing, and the private sector pay the cost of constructing, maintaining, and operating infrastructure. However, according to the Municipal Securities Rulemaking Boards, state and local governments own more than 90% of non-defense public infrastructure assets, which they finance primarily through the municipal securities market. Thus, another way to invest in infrastructure is by buying municipal bonds. A *municipal bond* is a debt obligation issued by a state or local government or one of its agencies or authorities such as a city or town. The issuer pays bondholders the principal plus interest over the bond's life, which can be 30 years or more. Individual retail investors, either directly or through municipal bond mutual funds, hold the vast majority of municipal bonds.

The two most common types of municipal bonds are general obligation (GO) and revenue bonds. A *GO bond* usually relies upon the bond issuer's full faith and credit to repay the bond. In contrast, a revenue bond typically relies on revenues from a specific project or system, such as a water or electric utility, to repay the bondholders. You can invest in these bonds directly or through municipal bond mutual funds and ETFs.

Municipal bonds offer both advantages and disadvantages. A major feature of most municipal securities is that bondholders' interest payments are exempt from federal and often state and local income taxes. They also have lower volatility than stocks and a high level of liquidity. If you buy municipal bonds in a mutual fund or ETF, you can reinvest bond income resulting in compound growth. Yet, municipal bonds have some drawbacks. For example, bond yields might not beat inflation, and the risk of default or loss of capital is a possibility. Municipal bonds are also subject to *interest rate risk*, which is the inverse relationship between interest rates and bond value. When interest rates go up, current bonds lose value. You face an opportunity cost by investing in a municipal bond because you could realize a higher return on a comparable taxable bond.

5.29. WHAT ARE THE TRADEOFFS BETWEEN INVESTING IN PUBLIC (LISTED) VERSUS PRIVATE (UNLISTED) INFRASTRUCTURE, SPECIFICALLY IN AN INFRASTRUCTURE PE FUND?

Several tradeoffs exist when deciding whether to invest in infrastructure with public versus private investment vehicles.

- *Diversification.* In terms of asset diversification, investing in listed infrastructure has an advantage because it allows you to diversify by asset type and geography. In contrast, the concentration of private infrastructure investments tends to occur in one area resulting in single-asset risk.

- *Liquidity*. Another advantage of investing in listed infrastructure investments is liquidity. You can withdraw funds according to your timeframe and fully invest your funds at one time. In contrast, if you invest in a PE infrastructure fund, your funds could be locked-up for several years with limited exit opportunities. Thus, you draw down your committed capital and invest it over time. Therefore, you can't invest all of your funds at once.

- *Fees*. Your fees are lower with a listed vehicle compared to an unlisted one. For example, PE firms charge both management and performance fees, which reduce your expected net returns. Although PE funds often invest in single infrastructure assets, they provide disclosure, which can be useful in conducting due diligence before investing.

5.30. WHERE IS A GOOD PLACE TO START INVESTING IN INFRASTRUCTURE FOR A TYPICAL INDIVIDUAL INVESTOR?

The typical investor interested in investing in infrastructure is more likely to start investing in public (listed) versus private (unlisted) infrastructure for the reasons just mentioned. Thus, the question remains what publicly-traded vehicle is most appropriate: common stock, listed mutual funds, ETFs, MLPs, or debt. Since each investment has advantages and disadvantages, you would have to examine how these tradeoffs relate to your investment objectives and constraints. Thus, no "one-size-all" answer exists.

Individual investors typically value their time and want to avoid the enormous amount of work needed to actively

manage a portfolio. Thus, they tend to migrate toward pro-
fessionally managed funds such as mutual funds and ETFs.
MLPs are probably off their initial radar. Although all three
investments have benefits and drawbacks, a good starting
point would be to consider an index infrastructure ETF. Next,
you need to decide whether you want exposure to stocks
globally or concentrate on holdings in the United States. You
want a fund with a historical record that closely tracks the
performance of its chosen index. As with other sector funds,
you'd be wise to use infrastructure ETFs as diversification
tools and not allocate all of your infrastructure allocations to
a single niche in the market.

5.31. WHAT TYPES OF INDIVIDUAL INVESTORS ARE INFRASTRUCTURE BEST SUITED?

Infrastructure investments are most attractive as part of a
long-term investment strategy. Thus, if you seek an investment with a potentially long-term, low-risk, and inflation-
linked profile, then investing in infrastructure could be right
for you. Adding infrastructure to a balanced portfolio could
also provide a new source of return and diversification of risk.
MLPs are popular investments for income-seeking investors
and those willing to deal with tax issues at tax time. MLPs
are suitable for taxable accounts, not retirement accounts,
because they're already tax-advantaged entities.

Although MLPs are a solid investment opportunity for
some people, they're not for everyone. Those who prefer
more straightforward investments may choose to buy stocks
or bonds – investments whose tax consequences aren't nearly
as complicated. Many consider MLPs as low-risk, long-term
investments, providing a slow but steady income stream.
Thus, they're an ideal source of retirement income.

When investing in infrastructure, investors typically look for a particular risk-return profile. For individual investors focusing on the long term and wanting to add infrastructure to their portfolios for the first time, a good starting point is to focus on those investments providing cash flow stability, which reduces potential risk. Thus, if you have a lower risk profile within the overall universe, you should focus on core and core-plus assets. Many regard these investments as defensive because they tend to provide a steady return throughout the investment cycle. However, some infrastructure investments tend to be a better fit for adventurous, risk-loving investors, such as the added-value and opportunistic asset segments. To achieve the goal of reducing cash flow volatility in your portfolio, you should allocate relatively small amounts to greenfield infrastructure and emerging markets.

5.32. WHAT ARE SOME USEFUL ONLINE RESOURCES FOR INFRASTRUCTURE?

Numerous websites offer information about investing in general and infrastructure in particular. Here are a few of them.

- Investopedia (https://www.investopedia.com) is a leading source of financial content on the web that focuses on investing and finance education and analysis.

- The Motley Fool (www.fool.com) provides investors with financial advice through various stock, investing, and personal finance services.

- Morningstar (https://www.morningstar.com/funds.html) provides a hub for mutual fund news, analysis, and data. It is best known for its "star rating" system, which is on a scale of one to five stars. This system offers help when choosing mutual funds.

- Lipper Leaders (http://www.lipperleaders.com/index. aspx) offers mutual fund information, analytical tools, and commentary. Lipper rates mutual funds relative to their peers and delivers an instant measure against five metrics, including total return, consistent return, preservation, expense, and tax efficiency.

- ETF.com (http://www.etf.com) offers authoritative news, analysis, and education about ETFs.

- Morningstar (https://www.morningstar.com/etfs.html) provides a hub for ETF news, analysis, and data.

- Alerian (https://www.alerian.com/education/resources/) provides extensive online materials involving investing in energy infrastructure and MLPs.

- Suredividend.com (https://www.suredividend.com/mlp-list/) provides a detailed discussion of MLPs and spreadsheet data updated daily.

TAKEAWAYS

Investing in infrastructure is off the well-trodden path of most individual investors who usually gravitate to traditional investments. Yet, savvy investors know that traditional and alternative investments provide complementary routes to building wealth over the long term. New investors often start with traditional investments. They then add alternative investments to their portfolios as they gain additional knowledge and experience. Infrastructure is simply one type of investment on the alternative investing menu. Although direct investment in infrastructure is often beyond the typical individual investor's reach, investing in listed infrastructure securities can add such potential benefits as greater diversification, liquidity, and lower fees. Investing in unlisted, illiquid firms with a long-term horizon also requires specialist knowledge and should typically lead investors to delegate this process to investment managers. Although some infrastructure investments can be dicey, the risk of a substantial loss of capital, aside from extraordinary events, is low with proper analysis. Here are some lessons from this chapter.

- Review your investment goals to ensure that investing in infrastructure is consistent with them.

- Start with broad-based investments such as indexed mutual funds and ETFs before focusing on individual stocks or bonds.

- Remember that infrastructure investments fit best as part of a long-term investment strategy.

- Make sure that infrastructure investments are compatible with your risk tolerance.

- Avoid high-risk infrastructure products unless you fully understand their specific risks and are willing to accept them.

- Be aware of the pros and cons of each type of infrastructure investment before investing.

- Be careful before investing in MLPs because, despite high yields, they involve many complications.

- Avoid investing in an infrastructure investment vehicle that you don't understand.

- Spread your money across different investment types and sectors that respond differently to what's happening in the economy.

- Check the costs associated with infrastructure investments and keep them low where possible.

- Keep track of how your investments are performing and make necessary adjustments to reach your financial goals.

- Heed the warning label: Don't assume an investment is likely to continue to do well in the future simply because it's done well in the past.

INDEX